A STUDY OF PETER CHELČICKÝ'S LIFE AND A TRANSLATION FROM CZECH OF PART ONE OF HIS NET OF FAITH

A Thesis
Presented to
the Faculty of the Department of Church History
Pacific School of Religion

In Partial Fulfillment
of the Requirements for the Degree
Bachelor of Divinity

by
Enrico C. S. Molnár
Berkeley, California, February 1947

Printed in the United States of America

0 1 2 3 4 5 6 7 8 9

First Printing, 2017

ISBN 978-1-941489-31-4

www.MetaphysicalPocketBooks.Com
www.AudioEnlightenment.Com

First "AudioEnlightenmentPress.com" Printing
August, 2017

Publishers Notes:

This PDF has been sitting in my computer for over 10 years now as I had come across a reference to it while narrating Tolstoys, *"Kingdom of GOD is within You"* where Tolstoy had been lamenting its obscurity and exposing the "conspiracy of silence" that surrounds this part of the Gospel 451 years after its initial publication.

I had hoped someone would publish a paperback version, and waited and waited, but alas no movement. It remained silently in the shadows of my computer as I researched lost spiritual classics for years. Then once again as I was researching some books I came across the PDF sitting there, silent in its repose, asking for nothing, expecting nothing, when I finally decided that someone had to take the initiative to bring this important work into the public's consciousness after 100's of years in virtual obscurity.

Then the question arose, publish for the academic / researcher or the general public? And what exactly would that entail?

Academics / Researchers love footnotes, annotations, citations, etc which makes for an incredible indepth read, but it is a choppy and non fluid read for the general public. Footnotes every other sentence is a distraction for most people and in today's society of already strained attention spans I chose to remove over 525 footnotes and clean up the text and pages for the general reader. This text has been available for the academic online for decades and I have included a link to the full foot noted edition at the end of the book for those that want to delve deeper in research.So I ask for the academics forgiveness as I format this for the general reader.

The next consideration is called recto, a formatting issue. In the west, every new chapter is supposed to start on the right side in a 2 page spread. Now with so many chapters which were only one page long, do we add several hundred extra blank pages to fulfill that requirement or save a few trees by making common sense editing where we see fit. I decided to save a few trees.

Special thanks to Enrico C. S. Molnar & Mr Tom Lock

Introduction

The two-fold aim of the following thesis is defined by its title: it presents a translation, from the Czech language, of a religio-political treatise called *The Net of Faith*, written sometime between 1440-1443 by Peter Chelčický, a yeoman from southern Bohemia, and a contemporary of the Hussite Revolution. Chelčický was the most original thinker of the Bohemian Reformation; today there are preserved over fifty writings of different lengths that came from his pen. His most mature and most representative work is *The Net of Faith*.

I consider this translation of *The Net* as the core of my thesis; to it I have prefaced several chapters in which I have endeavored to evaluate the significance of Peter Chelčický, to show his unique position in the Czech reformation, and to underscore his characteristic contribution to European Protestant religious thought.

In choosing this subject for my thesis I am conscious that I am also paying back a debt that I owe Chelčický; the reading of his book led me to the choice of my vocation. I am also aware that he and his work are literally unknown in what is loosely termed the West. (For that matter, and it is sad to admit, the whole ideological content of Czechoslovak Protestantism as well as the ecclesiastical history of the Slavic peoples remain, for the great part, an uncharted map to Anglo-American Protestantism, which is still often compelled to inscribe the blank spaces with the legend *hic sunt leones*.)

The Net of Faith consists of two parts: in the first part, composed of ninety-five chapters, Chelčický presents his basic philosophy; the second part, divided into fifty-one chapters, contains 'illustrative material' in elaboration of Part I. Even though this section is – from the literary point of view – by far most interesting in that it vividly portrays the different facets of medieval life, it is omitted in the present thesis. In translating I used the critical edition of Peter Chelčický's *Net of Faith* made by Dr. Emil Smetánka, Professor of Czech Language at Charles University, Prague; this I often compared with the facsimile reprint of the first printed edition of 1521, a copy of which is available in the Library of the University of California.

I am indebted to Professor George H. Williams of Starr King School for the Ministry, Berkeley, who read parts of the translation while it was in the process of growth, and who has made many helpful suggestions; to the editors of *The Moravian* for permission to use large portions of my article, "The Prehistory of Moravianism," which appeared in that magazine, and especially to my brother, Rev. Amedeo Molnár of Prague, who supplied me with much needed critical literature about Chelcický published in Bohemia during the war years, beside contributing many constructive suggestions. And finally, I owe many thanks to my wife who learned that helping with a thesis in many practical ways is essential in making marriage a success.

Table of Contents

List of Illustrations

Abbreviations

AT	The Complete Bible – An American Translation, Chicago: The University Press, 1941
KJ	The Holy Bible, King James Version
NF	The Net of Faith (this document)
RSV	The New Testament, Revised Standard Version, Revised 1946

Czech Pronunciation

Special symbols called diacritical marks are placed above standard characters to indicate sounds peculiar to Czech, which is a phonetic language that has only one sound for each letter. Emphasis is always on the first syllable and the diacritical marks do not change the way syllables are emphasized. When vowels appear together they are both sounded instead of being combined to form a diphthong. For example, the word 'mouth' would be pronounced 'moh-ooth'. Vowels with a diacritical mark are lengthened.

Czech Letter	English Sound	Examples / (Notes)
a, á	Ah	Mama
c	Ts	lets (never the 'c' sound in 'car')
č	Ch	Church
ch		auch (German), loch (Scottish)
Ď, ď	Dy	duke (British pronunciation – 'dyook')
e, é	Eh	Let
ě	Yeh	Yet
i	Ih	Sit
í	Eeh	Machine
j	Y	year, yard (never the 'j' sound in 'jar')
l	L	(sometimes preceded by a short 'uh' sound)
ň	Ny	tenure ('ten-yoor')
o, ó	Oh	Tone
r	R	(rolled slightly, sometimes preceded by a short 'uh' sound)
ř		(similar to the English 'r' followed by the 'ž' sound)
š	Sh	Ship
Ť, ť	Ty	tune (British pronunciation – 'tyoon')
u, ú, ů	Oo	Prune
y, ý		(same as 'i' and 'í')
ž	Zh	azure, pleasure

Notes about the Translation

The translator tried to put into modern English thoughts preserved in medieval Czech. In order to do this he felt he had to have liberty in translation and occasional license to paraphrase. As to the faithfulness to the Czech original, the translator endeavored not to commit major distortions of essential meanings. Where he felt it advisable to freely paraphrase a certain passage or to condense a section in his own words, he marked the beginning and end of each paraphrase by a pair of square brackets: [ ]. In particular, in chapters 24 to 95 Chelčický uses biblical grounds to controvert and expose the fallacy of some objections raised against his arguments. Since these chapters represent an elaboration of the previous material, the translator has presented only their short synopsis. Those portions that offer new insights into Chelčický's philosophy have been fully translated.

Notes about Cover Illustration

The net is held by four apostles and in the net are the righteous Christians. One sinner is falling overboard and another is escaping through a big hole in the torn net. Below, protruding from the open jaw of an infernal leviathan, the devil is roping in the pope, the emperor, the learned doctors, and other sinners.

From the frontispiece Illustration of the 1521 Edition of The Net of Faith

Printed in the Monastery of Vilémov

We had the image artistically redrawn to express the vivid imagery that the woodcut intended. Original Image page 40

Tolstoy on "The Net of Faith"

Soon after the publication of my book in German, I received a letter from a professor of the Prague University, which informed me of the existence of a still unpublished work by the Bohemian Chelčický, of the fifteenth century, by the name of *The Net of Faith*. In this work, as the professor wrote me, Chelčický about four centuries ago expressed the same view in regard to the true and the false Christianity, which I had expressed in my work, *My Religion*. The professor wrote to me that Chelčický's work was for the first time to be published in Bohemian in the periodical of the St. Petersburg Academy of Sciences. As I was unable to procure the work itself, I tried to become acquainted with what was known of Chelčický, and such information I got from a German book sent me by the same Prague professor, and from Pýpin's "History of Bohemian Literature."

This is what Pýpin says:

The Net of Faith is that teaching of Christ which is to draw man out from the dark depths of the sea of life and its untruths. True faith consists in believing in God's words; but now there has come a time when men consider the true faith to be heresy, and so reason must show wherein the true faith consists, if one does not know it. Darkness has concealed it from men, and they do not know Christ's true law.

To explain this law, Chelčický points out the original structure of Christian society, which, he says, is now regarded as rank heresy by the Roman Church.

This primitive church was his own ideal of a social structure, based on equality, freedom, and brotherhood. Christianity, according to Chelčický, still treasures these principles, and all that is necessary is, that society should return to its pure teaching, and then any other order, in which kings and popes are needed, would seem superfluous: in everything the law of love alone is sufficient.

Historically Chelčický refers the fall of Christianity to the times of Constantine the Great, whom Pope Sylvester introduced into Christianity with all the pagan customs and life. Constantine, in his turn, invested the Pope with worldly wealth and power. Since then both powers have been aiding one another and have striven after external glory. Doctors and masters and the clergy have begun to care only for the subjugation of the whole world to their dominion, have armed men against one another for the purpose of murdering and plundering, and have completely destroyed Christianity in faith and in life. Chelčický absolutely denies the right to wage war and administer capital punishment; every warrior and even "knight" is only an oppressor, malefactor, and murderer.

The same, except for some biographical details and excerpts from Chelčický's correspondence, is said in the German book.

Having thus learned the essence of Chelčický's teaching, I with much greater impatience waited for the appearance of *The Net of Faith* in the journal of the Academy. But a year, two, three years passed, and the book did not appear. Only in 1888 I learned that the printing of the book, which had been begun, had come to a stop. I got the proof-sheets of as much as had been printed, and I read the book.

The book is in every respect remarkable.

The contents are quite correctly rendered by Pýpin. Chelčický's fundamental idea is this, that Christianity,having united with the power in the time of Constantine and having continued to develop under these conditions, has become absolutely corrupt and has ceased to be Christianity. The title "The Net of Faith," was given by Chelčický to his work, because, taking for his motto the verse of the Gospel about calling the disciples to become fishers of men, Chelčický, continuing this comparison, says, "Christ by means of His disciples caught in His net of faith the whole world, but the larger fish, tearing the net, jumped out of it, and through the holes, which these larger fish had made, all the others went away, and the net was left almost empty."

The large fish that broke through the net are the rulers, emperors, popes, kings, who, in not renouncing their power, did not accept Christianity, but its semblance only.

Chelčický taught what has been taught until the present by the Mennonites and Quakers, and what in former years was taught by the Bogomils, Paulicians, and many others. He teaches that Christianity, which demands from its followers meekness, humility, kindness, forgiveness of sins, the offering of the other cheek when one cheek has been smitten, love of enemies, is incompatible with violence, which forms an indispensable condition of power.

A Christian, according to Chelčický's interpretation, can not only not be a chief or a soldier, but cannot even take part in the government, be a merchant or even a landowner; he can be only an artisan or an agriculturist.

This book is one of the extremely few that have survived the auto-da-fés of books in which the official Christianity is arraigned. All such books, which are called heretical, have been burned together with the authors, so that there are very few ancient works which arraign the departure of official Christianity, and so this book is especially interesting.

But besides being interesting, no matter how we look upon it, this book is one of the most remarkable productions of thoughts, as judged by the depth of its contents, and the wonderful force and beauty of the popular language, and its antiquity. And yet this book has for more than four centuries remained unprinted, and continues to be unknown, except to learned specialists.

One would think that all these kinds of works, by the Quakers, and Garrison, and Ballou, and Chelčický, which assert and prove, on the basis of the Gospel, that our world comprehends Christ's teaching falsely, ought to rouse interest, agitation, discussions, in the midst of the pastors and of the flock. Works of this kind, which touch on the essence of the Christian teaching, ought, it seems, to be analyzed and recognized as true, or to be rejected and overthrown. But nothing of the kind has happened. One and the same thing is repeated with all these works.People of the most different views, both those who believe and, what is most surprising, those who are unbelieving liberals, seem to have an agreement to pass them stubbornly in silence, and all that has been done by men to elucidate the true meaning of Christ's teaching remains unknown or forgotten.

Excerpt "The Kingdom of God Is Within You"
Leo Tolstoy
1893

Notes about the Transcription

It is truly a tragedy that Rev. Molnár did not fully translate *The Net of Faith*. Unfortunately, I know no Czech (my sincere apologies go to those who do – I am sure that I have made many mistakes), so the best that I can do is to reproduce what he left us. I have made minor corrections to the spelling and grammar while preserving the meaning of the text. This transcription is under no copyright protection. It is my gift to you. You may freely copy, print, and transmit it, but please do not change or sell it, and please inform me of mistakes so that I can correct them.

Why have I bothered to do this? The short answer is that the Holy Spirit told me it was important. Chelčický wrote The Net of Faith around 1443. 451 years later Tolstoy brought it to our attention in his *Kingdom of God is Within You*, lamenting its obscurity and exposing the "conspiracy of silence" that surrounds this part of the Gospel. It was another 53 years before Rev. Molnár made the first and only English translation, but his ultimate goal remained unfulfilled for 59 more years: his translation existed as a single copy – the original manuscript – in an academic library. Silence has reigned for 563 years. This is a part of my small effort to break the "conspiracy of silence."

Sadly, Chelčický wrote nearly six hundred years ago but we have not taken his words to heart. Too many Christians still "turn their whole mind to caring about comfort, licentious freedom, and temporal goods; to obtaining these things through cunning, increasing their profits through weal or woe, and gaining privileges from (those in authority) or winning those privileges back if lost. For all this they invent clever defenses and fortifications for warfare…" The Church is older but no wiser, and Protestant Denominations are now guilty of much that Chelčický railed against in the Roman Church. Those few of us who are like Peter Chelčický still long for a Church that is true to the gospel.

It is worth noting that in Chelčický I have not only a kindred-spirit, but a fellow-countryman as well. My father's family comes from the region around Chelčice – from an area extending 20 miles to the east and 45 miles to the northwest, to be exact – and has been traced back there to the late 1600s. It is entirely possible that my ancestors were personally inspired by Chelčický during his lifetime.

Finally, I would like to thank "my good friend in Pacifica" for making this transcription possible.

Tom Lock

Notable Quotations

Our faith obliges us to bind wounds, not to make blood run.

He who obeys God needs no other authority.

You cannot improve society without first destroying the foundations of the existing social order.

The Church rather likes a wicked king, for this man – if sufficiently intoxicated by her poisons – will fight for her better than a humble Christian.

Wars and other kinds of murder have their beginning in the hatred of the enemy and in the unwillingness to be patient with evil. Their root is in intemperate self-love and in immoderate affection for temporal possessions. These conflicts are brought into this world because men do not trust the Son of God enough to abide by his commandments.

Peter Chelčický – A Symbolical Pen Drawing

PART I

A HISTORICAL STUDY OF PETER CHELČICKÝ:

HIS LIFE, WORK, AND PHILOSOPHY

1

Chapter 1

What is the Net of Faith?

There is an oriental story that tells of a ruler who summoned wise men to his palace and asked them the question, "What thing, in the whole world, gives the most light?" The wise men answered, "The sun." Then the ruler asked, "What gives the most light when the sun is down?" The wise men replied, "The moon." – "And what if the moon is down and the sun not yet up; what is, then, the brightest thing in the world?" – "The stars."

And the ruler pressed on and on with his questions, eliminating the sun, the moon, the stars, the Taj-Mahal, and Aladdin's lamp, until the wise men got together and gave their final answer to the ruler: "Know thou, O most illustrious King, that there is no thing in the whole universe that gives more light than the soul of man."

If the Slavs were asked who their most illustrious men are, past and present, they would with one accord give a galaxy of names that would certainly include such immortals as Copernicus, Dostoyevsky, Tolstoy, Hus, Mickiewicz, Dvořák, Strosmayer, Comenius, Soloviev, Masaryk, Kosciuszko, Šafařík, Tchaikovsky…

If they were asked to name their profoundest philosopher, the answer would be Dostoyevsky.

If they were asked to name their best theologians, they would point to Berdyaev, Soloviev, and Comenius.

And if the question were, "Who is, among all Slavs, the most original thinker and the most radical Christian?" the consensus of opinion would certainly say, "Peter Chelčický!"

Peter Chelčický, born sometime toward the close of the fourteenth century in Southern Bohemia, during the days of John Hus' fame, became the most critical opponent of Romanism as well as of the Hussite Revolution. Relentlessly, he sought the Christian way of life and the Christian answer to the historical, social, and economic problems of his time. He did not find it in the Church of Rome or in the bloody protest against it, Hussitism.

It is customary to speak of two types of Continental Reformation: Calvinist and Lutheran. Yet there was still a third type, waiting for more scientific exploration: the Slav or, specifically, the Czech Reformation. It bears the deep imprint of three prophetic personalities: of John Hus, its protagonist, hero, and martyr; of John Amos Comenius, its philosopher, educator, and theologian; and of Peter Chelčický, its stern prophet, conscience, and climax. Hus appeals to our heart and imagination, Comenius appeals to our mind and thought, and Chelčický appeals to our soul and conscience. Hus is colorful and dramatic, Comenius is majestic and profound, and Chelčický is rugged and disturbing.

Both Hus and Comenius were highly educated men; they wrote in Czech as well as in Latin; their work was known abroad. Chelčický was born and remained the rest of his life a peasant, a yeoman. He did not possess an academic education and knew only the rudiments of Latin. He wrote only in Czech, and so it happens that his work is well nigh unknown in the West.

That Chelčický ranks among the most precious manifestations of the Czech mind is not only the exalted opinion of the writer of this thesis; all those who are conversant with Czech and Slav culture and literature concur. "Some Czech historians call Chelčický – and perhaps not without foundation – the greatest philosophic genius of his age in all coeval Europe." One of the first foreigners who became acquainted with the work of Chelčický, Leo N. Tolstoy, declared:

Apart from its interest, concerning which there may be differences of opinion, it is one of the most remarkable results of human thought, both on account of its profundity and the wonderful power and beauty of its language, not to mention its antiquity. And yet, this book has remained unprinted for centuries, and continues to be unknown except to a few specialists... This book is among the few that have been saved from the flames into which books denouncing official Christianity were commonly cast...

The Net of Faith is the doctrine of Christ, wherewith man is to be raised from the gloomy depths of the social sea of iniquity. True faith is to believe the word of God, but we are living in a time when men call the true faith heresy. Hence, it is upon our own reason that we must rely to discover truth if we possess it not. Darkness has concealed it from men and they no longer recognize the true law of Christ.

The first president of Czechoslovakia, Thomas Garrigue Masaryk, held a very high esteem for Chelčický, even though he did not agree with the radical implications of this philosopher's ethics:

Chelčický ... is a clear, absolutely consistent, and intrepid thinker and pioneer, an enemy of violence; he is Hus and Žižka in one soul, a man thoroughly Czech... Hus – Žižka – Chelčický – Comenius: what name can the Hapsburg Counter-Reformation muster against these names, sacred to the whole nation? Against a great idea it is able to muster only bare violence.

Ernest Denis, the French historian, writes in his history of the Hussite wars:

(Chelčický) était une âme tender et pieuse, pleine de foi, d'enthousiasme et de charité. On ne pouvait le connaître sans l'aimer... L'adoration de Dieu, cette charité qui ouvrent le ciel, on ne les impose pas, on ne commande pas l'amour; aussi Chelčický condamne-t-il de la manière la plus formelle toute violence et toute tyrannice .

Peu d'hommes ont donné lieu a autant de travaux et de controverses que Kheltchitsky (*sic*). Épreuve redoutable que ces examens répétés et ces polemiques: il en est sorti plus grand. A mesure qu'on le connaît mieux, on se prend pour lui d'une sorte de vénération attendrie. Chez lui, tout parle au coeur, parce que tout vient du coeur, la doctrine comme l'éloquence.

4

And speaking of the followers and disciples of Chelčický he writes:

L'histoire ne connaît peut-être pas de spectacle plus touchant que celui de ses communautés qui marchent pendant les siècles la main dans la main sans une pensée de révolte ou une parole de colère...

And on the American side, Dr. Matthew Spinka of Hartford Theological Seminary recently wrote a detailed evaluation of Peter Chelčický. He prefaced it with these words:

Among the outstanding figures of the period of the "flowering of the Czech Reformation," Peter Chelčický occupies a prominent, and in some respects a unique, position. Although not as well known as John Hus, from certain points of view Peter is more important, and certainly more original, than the great Czech Reformer, insofar as in his radical Biblicism he went far beyond the latter.

These estimates must suffice to show the eminent place reserved for Chelčický in all studies of the Czech Reformation. We shall deal with the life of Chelčický elsewhere; this thesis centers on his largest and most celebrated work, *The Net of Faith*. Chelčický was, however, a prolific writer reacting to all major issues of the day. The subjects of his books and treatises show the universality of his keen mind: they range from discussing theft and civil law to interpretations of the Lord's Prayer, St. Matthew's Gospel, and the Sacraments, and from a condemnation of the caste system to Sunday meditations.

Still, *The Net of Faith* remains his most mature work. This *magnum opus* has become, in many respects, the most important work of the Czech Reformation. Its language makes no easy reading and, so far, it has been translated only into two other languages, Russian and German.

The writer of this thesis has felt that this work should be made available to the English speaking public, especially to the student of Church history and religious thought. It is with a sense of great humility that he responded to the challenge of faith and assumed the task of translation.

Chapter 2

Peter Chelčický, The Setting In Time

In the primitive church the chalices were of wood, the prelates of gold; in these days the Church hath chalices of gold and prelates of wood.

– Girolamo Savonarola

Anno Domini 1500 – Sandro Botticelli finished painting that populous *Nativity* which is one of the chief attractions of the London National Gallery; over it may still be read the painter's own words in Greek: "This picture was painted by me Alexander amid the confusions of Italy at the time prophesied in the Second Woe of the Apocalypse, when Satan shall be loosed upon the earth."

Old Botticelli had never been outside the confines of his native Italy, hence he wrote of the "confusions of Italy." And truly a confused Italy it was; it was the Italy of the days when a cardinal could be known as the father of four children and yet be elected Pope; it was the Italy of the secularized princes of the Church and of municipal dictators, the Visconti and Sforza of Milan, the Scaligers of Verona, the Gonzagas of Mantua, and the Medici of Florence. The popes and the princes knew the difference between a good statue and a bad statue, but they knew not the difference between good and evil; they all fought each other in palace and in field, with daggers and with crosses, and many of them died of the disease of the age known as the tuberculosis of the Borgia: poison. In some city-states they employed artists as ambassadors, while in Rome the rabble became so noisy and dangerous that several Popes had to flee St. Peter's dilapidated city to save their bare skins. Botticelli was certainly justified when he put those Greek words into his Natività: "This picture was painted by me Alexander amid the confusions of Italy at the time prophesied in the Second Woe of the Apocalypse, when Satan shall be loosed upon the earth."

But had Botticelli visited the countries outside Italy, he would have had to write the same thing there; for there was confusion in France, confusion in Germany, in Bohemia, everywhere. England was absorbed in her War of the Roses; Spain was busy exterminating Indians in her newly discovered America, *para la mayor gloria de Dios*; Germany was in a state of chaos; in the West, France lay exhausted from a hundred years' struggle to drive the English from the continent, and just then was saved from utter defeat by the picturesque and dramatic appearance of a 19 year old village girl from the Vosges who "lectured, talked down, and overruled statesmen and prelates." In the South, a Pope was calling the curses of heaven down upon a second Pope who put up his headquarters at Avignon, and who retaliated in kind. In the East the Turks were knocking down the last fences of the Byzantine Empire, which had been kept alive only by repeated blood transfusions.

The fourteenth century, at the close of which Peter Chelčický was born, was a strange century indeed. It was an era of great social ferments, natural catastrophes, famines, plagues, and unusual men. In this period the ice drift cut off communication with Greenland, and the advancing glaciers almost literally pushed the settlements into the sea. European chroniclers of the century recorded two excessively cold winters. Crops failed in Norway and then in England and in France. There were excessive rains. The Sequoia tree rings in California ran to abnormal width, the Caspian Sea expanded, and the Rhine, the Danube, the Thames, and the Elbe froze. Fifty-five summers of this century saw violent floods and the Cathedral of Mayence was submerged to the famous frieze over the door. In the Netherlands seventy-two cities were destroyed by the sea in one night and 200,000 people were drowned in one year. The Black Death, the Asiatic Cholera, the Athenian Plague, and famine killed thirteen million people in China and reduced the populations of France and England by one third. The common people were impoverished, ill-fed, and ill-housed. Yet, at the same time the secular and ecclesiastic princes lived in a byzantinesque luxury that only accentuated their aloofness from the common *hoi polloi*. While the peasants complained that they "haue the payne and traveyle, rayne and wynd in the feldes," the doorways of the castle of Vincennes had to be raised in order to accommodate the three-foot tall head-dress of Isabelle of Bavaria.

A rigid caste system, perpetuating itself by a ruthless exploitation of the common people, was entrenched on the whole continent of Europe, upheld by secular powers and sanctioned *urbi et orbi* by the Church. The iron hand of authority and the cramped hand of plague were the two clutches which held Europe in a deadly embrace.

However, by a strange twist of fortune, Bohemia was spared – for a while at least – of all these Egyptian plagues. It was soon recognized that the rich seemed to be unaffected by the diseases; for they did not live in the over-populated cities and unhygienic suburbs of the poverty-stricken plebeians. At any rate, under the rule of the Luxembourg Emperor Charles IV (*regnavit* 1346-1378 as Karel I), Bohemia reached its peak of economic wealth and prosperity, and the King-Emperor inaugurated a new policy of tearing down old overcrowded city slums and building completely new districts, particularly in Prague, with wide streets, vineyards, and spacious palaces. Perhaps this sanitary urban reconstruction was one of the reasons why the plague stayed away so long from Bohemia (it appeared there only during the Thirty Years' War). Of course, the contemporaries did not explain it that way. They found their answer rather in supernatural phenomena. It became a common belief that Bohemia was under a special protection of God and St. Wenceslas, with the result that all the rich nobles of the entire continent, desirous of enjoying the cultural life in the Emperor's capital and to escape at the same time the sword of Damocles continuously hanging over their plague-infested towns, flocked in droves to Bohemia. All this glory, prestige, and material wealth gave rise to many kinds of abuses and to a general moral decadence. The Church was thoroughly enmeshed in this demoralization. The Bohemian Church of that day possessed, for instance, not only extensive rights, but also one half of the entire area of the country.

It was precisely at this moment of crisis that Bohemia heard the prophetic voices of protest, hurled from the pulpits and housetops by Konrad Waldhauser (+1369), John Stěkna (+1369), Matthew of Janov (+1394), Milíč of Kroměříž (+1374), and particularly John Hus (+1414). The results, finally crystallizing in the popular upsurge of the Hussite movement, are too well known to be discussed here. Suffice it to say that after the martyrdom of John Hus his followers had honestly done away with the worst offences of the Church of Rome, but in the process of doing so they supplanted the tyranny of Rome with the two contending tyrannies of Prague and Tábor.

There was a quaint habit among certain Roman Emperors as well as among many famous men of this time to spend the last years of their 'pensioned' lives tenderly raising cabbages after they had spent a lifetime killing off their fellow men. Chelčický had no such distinguished past; he had his own small cabbage patch and he would have liked to tend to his plowshare and pruning hooks to the end of his life, had he not been born in an age of political turmoil and moral crisis.

While Bohemia was being torn by internecine religious warfare, Chelčický quietly plowed his fields and watched with concern the storms of wrath ravaging the similar fields of his neighbors and the fields and pastures of peasants all over Europe. He became intensely interested in history and its meaning, and especially in the Christian answer to history. He sought the answer in the Bible and he came to a conclusion which challenged the whole Hussite philosophy of life; it became unmistakably clear to him that there are only two choices before men: either they make life have meaning, a single purpose, comprehensive enough to embrace every human activity and worthy of man's highest achievement, or life will end them. He saw no middle course left. And a meaning as comprehensive as that can come only from a life that has its basis beyond time. If we were to put Chelčický's challenge into a modern framework he would say to us, "The Kingdom of God is a reality here and now, but can be realized completely only beyond history. We are a colony of heaven and as such, not bound by the earthly laws. Only by responding to God's agapé, by doing His will, no matter how much this Divine will conflicts with human ratiocinations, are we citizens of that transcendental Kingdom of God." "Love and do as you please," says St. Augustine; we are not bound to obey the laws of the kingdoms of this earth if we obey the transcendent, eternal laws; we are slaves of this world only because of our sinful nature. The transcendent Kingdom of God is here, now, yes, cutting across our immanent world of reason and power, but we can never completely free ourselves from the immanent "enslavement" except beyond history. We must improve society – and we can – but at best it will always remain an image of the Kingdom of God. It will not become the Kingdom itself.

To have a picture of things, a design for living adequate to embrace and coordinate all our experiences, we must have a perspective so vast that the point where all lines meet is eternity. Nothing can really be changed in time unless the fulcrum of that change is eternity.

Chelčický saw with his keen analytical mind that his contemporary Hussites – and the majority of Christians, for that matter – sought the 'fulcrum of change' not in eternity but in time, endeavoring to bring it about by an infallible legislation, by a rationalistic immaculate perception, and by compulsion. If the Church is to live up to its pretensions, he taught, it must be in the hands of God, and not God in the hands of the Church. Yet, precisely the latter was the official position of the Pope at Rome as well as of the Archbishop Primate of Prague and the Generalissimo of Tábor. Chelčický would have been amply justified to inscribe his work, with apologies to Botticelli, "This *Net of Faith* was written by me Peter amid the confusions of Bohemia and Europe, at the time prophesied in the Second Woe of the Apocalypse, when Satan, whose one horn is Protestant and the other Catholic, shall be loosed upon the earth."

Chapter 3

Peter Chelčický, His Life

I see no good in having several lords;

Let one alone be Master, let one alone be King.

– Homer

The curious case of Peter Chelčický is one of the much covered-up mysteries of the history of the Church and / or religious thought, in spite of the fact that "his works of outstanding quality in contents and in composition ... rank among the most precious manifestations of the Czech spirit." He has passed by acclamation into the company of the great philosophers of the Christian community on the strength of a total of some forty theological writings, and more particularly on the strength of his crowning magnum opus, *The Net of Faith*.

We know exceedingly little about him beyond what his writings and the correspondence of his contemporaries as well as what some of their oblique references disclose; though scholars have searched incessantly during the past three decades for any scrap of further information concerning so notable a figure.

There has been much conjecture as to where and when Peter Chelčický was born. There are two general theories. Until recently, the consensus of scholars was that the date of his birth should be sought in the year 1390 – or possibly sooner – but definitely not later. In other words, he was supposed to have been born sometime in the middle of the reign of King Václav IV of the Luxembourg Dynasty. According to this theory, his birthplace is to be found in Chelčice, a village not very far from Vodniany and Husinec (the birthplace of John Hus) in the region where, fifteen decades before, Peter Waldo presumably died. To his friends he was known as Brother Peter; and if this theory is correct, he began to call himself "Chelčický" after the village of Chelčice only in his thirties.

Quite recently Dr. F. M. Bartoš of the Hus Theological Seminary in Prague has come out with a new theory. Recalling the historian Palacký's hypothesis that Chelčický was a yeoman, Bartoš seeks to trace him in the documents relating to the country nobility, for only such background would explain the personal independence that Chelčický enjoyed, not being compelled to perform manorial duties. As far as we know, Chelčický never signed his works, and his name appears only later, on the printed volumes of his *Postilla* and *The Net of Faith*, that is, in the years 1522-1532, which is quite some time after his death. Master Příbram calls him, in 1443, simply "Peter." The appellation "Peter Chelčický" was possibly created by Brother Gregory of the Unitas Fratrum who visited Peter, toward the end of his life, in Chelčice. These considerations make a *tabula rasa* for the daring new theory of Bartoš who writes that Chelčický's original name may have been Petr Záhorka. His father was Svatomár of Záhorčí who claimed Hrádek Březí near Týn above the Moldau as his ancestral castle. This Peter was born sometime between 1374-1381. The documents describe him as a mild-mannered nobleman of a peaceful character who was not opposed to the secular legal order, "and it is worth noticing that Peter (Záhorka) joined the Táborites during the revolution... Peter Záhorka ceases to be mentioned in our sources after the year 1424 when he would have been at the most fifty years old...
But the disappearance of the news about Peter Záhorka could be also explained in this way, that his following existence continued in the life of Peter Chelčický."

If the hypothesis of Dr. Bartoš is correct, then we would venture to suggest the following reconstruction. The young 'Chelčický' was a scion of a family interested in politics and church life; this would explain a certain cultural maturity of the environment. He became orphaned in his early youth, thus losing a greater part of his inheritance. He was contemptuous of the customary career of his contemporaries and refused to enter the services of either the nobility or the Church, choosing instead to serve the people whom he wanted to educate.

13

If Chelčický were really Peter Záhorka, we would gain a valuable aid for the solution of the question as to when and how he arrived at his conclusions about the basic discrepancy between the principles of Christianity and the principles of the state. For, as we well know, he developed this theory ... only sometime around 1425 in his tract *About the Threefold People*.

The question of his occupation is not yet definitely settled either. The historian Šafařík thought that Chelčický was a priest, Lena assumed that he was a member of the Waldensian Church and even of a Waldensian family; later sources identify him as belonging to the cobbler's trade; other guesses range from regarding him a serf to a squire. On one occasion, Chelčický calls himself a peasant. This was often interpreted literally but it is hardly possible to think of him as a serf. Sedláček already sought him among the noblemen of Chelčice, while Chaloupecký argued that the views, peculiar knowledge, and traditions manifested in the writings of Chelčický identify him as belonging to the class of country squires.

This only corroborates the hypothesis of Bartoš. All available evidence seems to point in the direction of such a conclusion. In discussing Chelčický's special position, Professor Spinka writes:

Judging from his obvious sympathy and identification of himself with the common people, it seems fairly safe to assume that he was one of them; for had he been a serf, he would not have been free to go to Prague to study and later to devote himself to his literary work of religious reformation as he did.

Chelčický had no regular academic education; many of his adversaries took advantage of this fact reproaching him that he "not a priest, mingled into questions pertaining to priests only"; another shocking fact perturbed his more academic adversaries, namely, that he did not write in Latin, and what was worse, that he knew only the rudiments of that language! But he was humble in spirit and frankly confessed, "I can give but meager and weak testimony concerning Latin." The editor of the Vilémov Edition of *The Net of Faith* (1521) reminds us that "there are many who do not slight Chelčický just because he is a layman and not learned in the Latin tongue"; on the contrary, he emphasizes that though he was not a master of the seven arts, he certainly was a practitioner of the eight beatitudes and of all the divine commandments, and was therefore a real Czech Doctor, versed in the law of the Lord without aberration from the truth.

It is entirely possible that Chelčický studied in his youth in some monastery where he may have acquired an elementary knowledge of Latin. Whatever his academic background may have been, his correspondence and writings reveal that he was by all standards a man thoroughly acquainted with the crisis of his time and with the thought of the leading spirits of the contemporary scene, as well as with the literary heritage and history of the Christian Church.

Southern Bohemia where Chelčice is situated had been for quite some time the cradle of many men outstanding in religious thought of the fourteenth century, such as Matthew of Janov, Thomas of Štítný, Adalbert Raňkov, and others. It was a region "infested with Waldensian heresies," which found open doors of hospitality in the homes of humble peasants and small yeomen.

As to the physical aspect of the region, even today the voice of Southern Bohemia is rather on the quiet side; inarticulate, low-pitched, prone to the expression of humorous doubts and biting skepticism, rolling like the hills and meadows of the unpretentious countryside. There is nothing grandiose about this landscape: no snowcapped mountains but only furrowed fields, no broad rivers but only quiet brooks and placid lakes reflecting the skies.

Such is the region where – perhaps – Chelčický was born and where he certainly spent the latter part of his life. He seems never to have quitted Bohemia for a day during his seventy (or ninety) years of life; he went several times to Prague (where he may have heard John Hus), to Písek, and probably once to Kutná Hora. The excited social and political activities of these cities left him unmoved, and he gave greater preference to the contemplative solitude of Chelčice.

15

Among the earliest sources of Peter's knowledge were the writings of Thomas of Štítný. Their study left a deep imprint in Chelčický's spiritual life. Štítný's works, written in the vernacular, introduced him to the intellectual world of the Middle Ages, and the author's religio-ethical essays encouraged his alert mind to ponder and meditate over the basic Christian truths, to compare the ideals of the Church of the days of the Apostles and Fathers with the realities of the Christian Society of his own time, and to come to rather distressing and uncomplimentary conclusions.

The other three great influences on the intellectual development of Peter were John Hus, John Wyclif, and the Waldensian tradition. It is still a mooted question whether Chelčický ever met Hus in person but this we know for sure: he was thoroughly conversant with the writings of the great Czech reformer. Similarly, he knew the teachings of Wyclif with whose thought he became acquainted through various translations and extracts published in Prague as well as through the polemical literature flowing in abundant profusion from the pens of Hussite priests. And as to the third influence, "Waldensian heresies were rampant" all over southern Bohemia. In his opposition to Hussite formalism Chelčický could not but feel sympathetic toward the Waldensian teachings that urged a return to apostolic simplicity. In the following chapters we shall see how these ideas permeate his philosophy.

But Chelčický was not a copyist. Far from that. He accepted from Štítný, Hus, Wyclif, and Waldensianism what he thought to be sound and biblically correct; that was his starting point. But from there he went on quite independently, basing himself solely on the Bible. He disagreed with Štítný, who thought that a mere reform would do away with social injustices. "You cannot improve society without first destroying the foundations of the existing social order," insisted Chelčický. He felt a deep respect for Hus, but he rejected with harsh words his unbiblical notions of purgatory, his views on war, oaths, and the worship of pictures. He loved Wyclif but he rejected his traditional – can we say, 'undemocratic'? – division of men into three estates (lords, priests, and the working people). He felt very close to the Waldensians, but to him their Christianity was not radical enough. He agreed with St. Ambrose that God has given the earth to the common use of all, and that therefore the

16

rich have no exclusive right of ownership. He retained an astonishing independence of judgment that brought him into personal contact with the leading spirits of the Hussite movement. There is preserved an amazing woodcut of the period portraying Peter Chelčický discoursing on equal terms with the doctors of the Prague University; he had discussions with Master Jakoubek of Stříbro, head of the University, with the Hussite bishops Nicholas of Pelhřimov and John of Rokycana, who was then the Primate of Bohemia, and with the foremost Hussite philosopher Dr. Stanislav of Znojmo.

Peter Chelčický Conversing with the Doctors of the University of Prague(A photographic copy of a drawing reproduced in *Traktáty Petra Chelčického: O trojím lidu; O církvi svaté*, edited by Dr. Rudolf Holinka, Prague: Melantrich, 1940)

His unique position of independent spiritual leadership is attested by the custom that developed among all learned Czechs to send to him their writings or at least extracts of their books, requesting his criticism and judgment. Bishops and theologians journeyed to visit him at his farm in Chelčice or in the more convenient nearby town of Vodniany, and he in turn was invited to attend Táborite or Utraquist church councils at Písek, Kutná Hora, and elsewhere. His farmhouse soon became a refuge and oasis of all free-minded souls. When Peter Payne, the English "Hussite" theologian, was driven out of Prague after the restoration of Emperor Sigismund, he was welcomed in the hospitable solitude of Chelčický's home.

Of course, Chelčický was sought by these philosophers and theologians only after he had established his reputation as an independent thinker in 1419 when many of the more radical Hussites, the Táborite priests, impatient with the coming of the Kingdom of God "beyond history" and restive under chiliastic hopes, began to realize the Kingdom "in history" with sword in hand. It was then that Chelčický made public his first disagreement with the official position of Táborite Hussitism. We shall deal in the next chapter with the history of his estrangement from the Hussite movement; however, 1419 marks a decisive turn in Chelčický's life and deserves a closer study.

In that year it became apparent that an armed conflict between the supporters of Rome and the followers of Hus was inevitable. Together with other travelers from southern Bohemia, Chelčický went to Prague to take part in a popular gathering held in a place called "na Křížkách." When we examine the records of this gathering, which bears all the earmarks of a popular referendum or town-hall meeting, we cannot but be impressed by the concern the delegates of southern Bohemia felt about the whole question of justification of war. They asked whether it is permissible for Christians to attack an enemy "if necessity arises." The questions were addressed to the Masters of the Prague University – then a stronghold of Hussite learning. The Masters were decidedly embarrassed by such ill-timed questions. Jakoubek of Stříbro, the rector of the University and spiritual leader of the Hussite movement after Hus' martyrdom, answered on their behalf in the affirmative, imposing the condition that "all cruelty, avarice, and all iniquity and excess be eliminated." Chelčický was not satisfied, with this ambiguous answer. After the meeting he called on Jakoubek in his apartment near the Bethlehem Chapel, asking him to give scriptural evidence from the New Testament supporting war "short of cruelty and avarice." Jakoubek could supply no such "proof from the Gospel"; he was able to appeal only to the authority of the Church Fathers and to Thomas Aquinas' doctrine of the righteous war, a doctrine that sanctions war if it meets the three conditions of *causa iusta, auctoritas principis,* and *intentio recta.*

Chelčický found the arguments of Jakoubek unconvincing and the doctrine of Thomas Aquinas unacceptable. Chelčický became a nonconformist when he declared, "God never revoked His commandment 'You shall not kill'."

This reply is striking in its simplicity, consistency, and moral logic. In it Chelčický aligns himself with the traditional early Christian position of thorough pacifism. He takes up the absolutist stand of Tertullian who asserted that "Christ in disarming Peter unbelted every soldier." Chelčický was utterly disgusted with the dualistic ethic of Jakoubek and his fellow theologians of the Hussite Reformation, a dualism which anticipated formally and emotionally the principles adopted in 1643 by Cromwell's Ironsides, a dualism which tended to make the temporal power brutal and the spiritual power irresponsible, a dualism which gave its sanction to a special ethic for the *civitas Dei* and another for the *civitas terrena.*

Jakoubek became incensed by Chelčický's "obstinacy" and in 1420, when Emperor Sigismund declared war, which Pope Martin V seconded by proclaiming a crusade against "the Wyclefites, Hussites, and other heretics, their furtherers, harborers, and defenders," the masters of the University fully endorsed Jakoubek's Thomistic sanction of the "just war." It was on this occasion that Peter parted with the Calixtine leaders.

On both sides, papal and Hussite, war became not only outwardly but also ideologically a crusade. Hussitism was transformed into a reincarnation, as it were, of the primitive Hebrew concept of the Warrior Nation fighting

19

the battles of its War God Yahweh. It was quick, violent, and single-minded as are all true mass revolutions under which the old order crumbles to dust. And it was a crusade for Yahweh. For "a revolution always has this in common with a crusade: that it is fought not under but against the authority of the prince. A war fought primarily for the defense of an ideal tends to be a crusade, especially if that ideal is religious."

Hussitism proclaimed (allegiance) with the old Hosts of the Lord and against the violence of evil forces set violence for the good. An eye for an eye! The name of Jesus – the Prince of Peace – was sung by the thousands of warriors of Hussite columns with a fervor almost unheard of for fourteen hundred years, and the hands of the same people were still warm and red from the blood of the enemies of the Law of God:

> So then, archers and lancers of knightly orders,
> Halberdiers and scourge-bearers of all ranks,
> Remember the generous Lord,
> Fear no enemies and disregard their numbers.
> Have your Lord alone in your hearts,
> Fight with Him and for Him,
> And never flee before the enemy!...
> Shout joyously the war cry:
> "Onward ho! Up and at them!"
> Hold firm your weapons and cry:
> "God is our Lord!"

Chelčický realized with more penetrating insight than any other reformer the necessity for the Church of Christ of resisting identification with any organized company of people, that is, of being in a strict sense the fellowship of the Holy Spirit – the living spring of Christian life. With prophetic perception he revealed and denounced the Hussite tendency of identifying Christianity, the cause of Christ, with the cause of the Czech nation. He saw that to the iniquity of a crusade they added the curse of nationalism. This nationalism began with a sense of exclusion, or "manifest destiny," and ended with a desire for domination.

The fusion of the "sour ferment of nationalism" with the "new wine of democracy" in the "old bottles of tribalism," to use Toynbee's terminology, produced amazing immediate results. The Hussites, under the remarkable leadership of the warlord Žižka (who shares with the Timurid Emperor Babur of Northern India the dubious honor of inventing the fortified chariot that anticipates our modern tank) defeated the Imperial Crusaders' international brigades in two bloody battles near Prague.

Peter Chelčický's spiritual maturity and greatest intellectual activity coincided with these years of Czech military glory, the Hussite armies were fighting victoriously against almost all European nations; the fear and fame of these 'warriors of God' were so great that by the mere singing of their anthem they drove away the strong forces of crusaders sent against them (Julian Cesarini, the Papal Legate who later became famous at the Council of Basel, being on one occasion in such a hurry that he lost his purple mantle, his crucifix, and the pontifical bull, near Domažlice). Chelčický remained unswayed by the elation of the other Czechs joyously marching to the tune of their martial hymn, thinking they were establishing the Kingdom of God on earth. He severed his connection both with the masters of the Prague University and with the Táborites, and retired to his farm in Chelčice. He chilled the enthusiasm of the Hussites by telling them they were not a whit better than common murderers. To Žižka's fighters as well as to the University's scholars his Christian protest sounded like a discordant note in the martial strains of their anthem. Yet this did not deter Peter. He set himself apart from the national revolution and from the great struggles within the Hussite movement, concentrating all his efforts on the purification of the spiritual revolution started by John Hus. After his withdrawal to Chelčice he began his life mission to "enshrine his thoughts in works that rank among the most precious treasures of Czech literature." In all of them, regardless of their topic, he kept on reminding the followers of Hus that they cannot bring about the Kingdom of Heaven as long as a hell of hatred burned within their hearts.

In all of his writings we recognize his great debt to the men he admired: Wyclif, Hus, and Štítný. But he went further than any of these. In accordance with the Waldensian teachings, Chelčický proclaimed that the

21

taking of life in any form, even in war, was sin, and that whoever killed a man in battle was guilty of "hideous murder."

He felt the burden of the Lord and His Word was upon him and he looked at the Hussite affairs and the affairs of the world through the eyes of the Bible. Focusing his attention to the Kingdom which is not of this world, Chelčický returned time and again to the kingdoms of men, and not even the most modern and most daring thinkers ventured to postulate with such relentless and thoroughgoing logic the claim of the sovereignty of the rule of God over the affairs of the human society as did the wizard of Chelčice.

In the books which he began writing at his country retreat we sense a passionate popular protest against the cruel moral irresponsibility of the Hussites dependent for their intellectual priming on nothing more reliable than university professors suffering from acidosis of the head and heart, and against the similarly cruel ignorance of the crusaders who depended for their ethical balance on the immaculate perception of the Pope of Rome. He wrote these protests in a popular style often circumlocutious, sometimes involved, but always of such a quality that they remain "among the few medieval literary works which can even today captivate our interest."

A Printed Page from the 1521 Edition of *The Net of Faith*

(The section shows the beginning of the thirty-second chapter. At the end of the second line and beginning of the third line are the words "Mistr Protiva" – *i.e.* the "Master Adversary" – which stands for John Wyclif.)

Because of his high moral integrity and new approach to Biblical Christianity he gathered around himself a small group of loyal followers who were called the "Brethren of Chelčice." They distinguished themselves by being absolute pacifists who, by their insistence on unconditional obedience to the commandment "you shall not kill", dissociated themselves entirely from the patriotic Hussite wars; they refused to sanction capital punishment, to make oaths, and to accept any government position, thus in many features paralleling the Rhinelandish Brethren of the Free Spirit, the Dutch Brethren of the Common Life, the Mennonites, the Fratricelli, and anticipating the British Quakers.

In 1434 there occurred an event that led indirectly to the foundation of the Moravian Church or, as it is more accurately called, the Unity of Brethren: the Battle of Lipany. In this great fratricidal battle of the two Hussite factions, the radical Táborites were defeated by the moderate and aristocratic faction of the Utraquists. The consequence of this tragic event was a general religious tiredness and torpidity. The moderate Utraquism did not muster enough courage to settle accounts with the Church of Rome or to eradicate abuses within its own ranks of clergy. The Utraquist Archbishop, John of Rokycana, preached vehemently against this degeneration of the movement; he soon had the following of a small group of young men who strove after a purified Church life. These earnest seekers asked the Archbishop to advise them what to do in order to accomplish this reform. Jan Blahoslav, the historian of the Czech Brethren, recorded in 1547 Rokycana's answer:

Then Master Rokycana showed to those who were with him – which is to say, to Brother Gregory and other companions of his – the writings of Peter Chelčický, (admonishing them) to read these books which he himself often perused, especially since Peter Chelčický had written some of them especially to Master Rokycana. Obeying his advice the brethren read the books of said Peter Chelčický with much diligence. Yes, they even had many talks with him... And as soon as they saw again Master Rokycana they thanked him for his advice, and also, that they made very good use of it, they told him.

By this time Chelčický had already established his reputation as an independent thinker; in addition, he and Rokycana had exchanged a number of letters in which they discussed matters of ecclesiastical discipline, sacraments, and articles of faith. Even though they did not see eye to eye on many points, Rokycana – at that time, anyway – respected Chelčický's views, hence his recommendation to the young reformists to get in touch with the philosopher of Chelčice.

We do not know what Brother Chelčický spoke about with Brother Gregory and the "other companions of his," but we know that the result of these conversations was the establishment of a religious community on the estate of Castle Litice in the Eagle Mountains of northeastern Bohemia. This estate was a personal property of a Hussite nobleman, George of Podiebrad, who had just then become King of Bohemia.

(Gregory and the brethren) asked Rokycana to plead for them with the King that he might give them a place to live on his estate of Litice, in the village of Kunvald behind Žamberk. He granted their request and so many of the faithful gathered there...

Kunvald became the first community of the new growing "mustard seed." When King George had given them the grant, there gathered in Kunvald, under the outstanding leadership of Gregory, noblemen and artisans from Prague, and yeomen, priests and peasants from Moravia. All of them, forgetting their provenience and antecedents, began addressing each other "brother."

Brought together by their common yearning after the "City of God," they formally founded in 1457 the Unity of Brethren, and ten years later, in not far-away Lhotka near Rychnov, the *Unitas Fratrum* definitively broke away both from the Church of Rome and the Utraquist Church by inaugurating a priesthood of its own.

Peter Chelčický, strictly speaking, did not found the Church of the Unity of Brethren nor any other ecclesiastical organization; never did he become as famous as his older contemporary, John Hus. However, in solitude, and wearied by the atmosphere of strife and hatred, he grappled with the

25

problems of the gospel of Christ with a peasant-like tenacity which overcame all possible educational handicaps; amid the treacherous sands of time he found God who stands still; in the desert places of history he found the inner spring whose waters never fail; and he truly became a voice crying in the wilderness, an Amos of Bohemia who interpreted with audacious consistency the categorical imperative of Christian ethics to harmonize the means with the ends, the conduct of man with the all-pervasive Kingdom of God. He was one of those great individualists to be found in epochal periods, who gather to themselves the influence of preceding ages, and give new direction to the spiritual trends of succeeding generations.

Es bildet ein Talent sich in der Stille,Sich ein Charakter in dem Strom der Welt.

Chelčický himself was fortunate to live long enough to see the establishment of the Church of the Unity of Brethren; he may fairly well be called the spiritual father and founder of this new church, since it was his influence which was so decisive in shaping the thoughts and acts of the first Brethren, even though he never became an active participant in the founding of the Unity.

The day of his death is shrouded in a cloud of uncertainty, just as his birthday is unknown. He is supposed to have died sometime in 1460, in the days of King George of Podiebrad. With him died a representative of the purest ideals of the Middle Ages, a son of a great time, yet standing far above it. In that rugged expression of Christian faith he is a worthy successor in that noble line of Peters: Peter the Apostle who exclaimed, "We must obey God rather than men," and Peter Waldo who echoed him and, in pursuing this higher loyalty, dared to deny the man-made allegiance to Rome. We suggest it is no arrogance to place Peter Chelčický in this "apostolic succession" of the aristocracy of the spirit, because in an atmosphere of the despotism of uniformity – whether of the church or state variety – he dared to postulate and define the imperative need of refashioning human economics on the model of the early Church and of Christ's gospel of love.

Peter Chelčický is great, one of those "who shall inherit the earth," because he was humble, poor in spirit, and because, surrounded on all sides by the forces of the sword, he dared to break his own.

Chapter 4

Peter Chelčický and the Hussite Reformation, the Parting of the Ways

Hate everything that hinders love.

– Hans Denck

The story of Chelčický's growth to independence is a chapter in which we are still missing several links. At the present day, the available and known material enables us the reconstruction of his gradual estrangement from the Hussite Reformation in approximately the following sequence:

The Estrangement from the Táborites

In another place we spoke of the year 1419, which was so decisive in Chelčický's life. This was the year in which there occurred the initial rift with the Táborites because of his insistence on total non-violence. You will remember that he then asked the masters of the Prague University the question whether it is permissible for Christians to take part in war. He was not satisfied with their conservative answer, and became disappointed especially in Master Jakoubek of Stříbro, then head of the University, who had formerly maintained a pacifist position.

The issue of non-violence was still a matter of public discussion in 1421 in which year Chelčický wrote his pacifist contribution *O boji duchovním* (About the Spiritual Warfare), and a little later, *O církvi svaté* (About the Holy Church). These writings were addressed to the Táborites and were considerably read by them as well as by the growing circle of his followers. "They are the first books which we have preserved of the new nascent community." In his book *About the Spiritual Warfare*, written as an exposition of Ephesians 6: 10-20, wherein the Christian is exhorted to put on the whole armor of God," for his "warfare is not against flesh and blood, but against the principalities, ... against the spiritual hosts of wickedness in heavenly places," Chelčický shows how long he identified himself with the teachings and endeavors of the "Táborite Brethren" until the day when, incited by excessive chiliastic notions, they began an extermination war against all "unfaithful ones." By doing this they vitiated precisely those principles he cherished most, and he began to doubt the ethical justification of their position. Here, for the first time as far as we know, Chelčický expounded the fundamental pacifist thesis that a Christian must abstain from physical war and violence, since his main duty is the "spiritual warfare" against the evils of this world, violence being one of those evils.

The events of the year 1422 add weight to the "Záhorka" theory discussed earlier. For in this year there was held in Písek a convocation of the Táborites at which occasion a first major disagreement between the Táborites and General John Žižka is recorded. Disturbed by these unfortunate events, many of the leading Hussites went to see Chelčický whose influence was then already gaining momentum. The Záhorka theory lends plausibility to the startling spectacle of the most important spiritual leader of the Táborites, Bishop Nicholas of Pelhřimov, going way out to visit Chelčický. The memorable (meeting) took place in Vodniany, a small county seat near Chelčice. They discussed theological questions concerning the Eucharist while they were "sitting on the pond-dike." The purpose of the bishop "was to convince Chelčický that they (the Táborites) had nothing in common with the sect of the Beghards as they had been accused." Without this theory it would be more difficult to explain why the "grand old man" of Tábor deemed it necessary to have Chelčický (Záhorka?) accurately informed on theological minutiae. Otherwise, why should a mighty bishop be concerned about the opinions of a particular peasant in a wretched forgotten coign of Bohemia?

This meeting gave Chelčický the impetus to write his tractate *O čtyřech bytech* (About the Four Essences), addressed to the Táborite clergy, "a document memorable because of its disorientation in the question of the

Eucharist, but even more because of its slow emancipation from the Táborite Eucharistiology."

This book and the previous writings caused quite a stir; the Táborites were saying that Chelčický was busying himself in a denigration of their theology. Therefore, Bishop Nicholas and Václav Koranda invited Chelčický to come to Písek. The latter accepted the invitation and during their conversation in Písek Chelčický admitted that he was too harsh in his judgment. The Bishop gave him some of his Latin writings as well as other works held as authoritative by the Táborites. Afterwards, in studying the Bishop's writings, Chelčický came to the realization that Bishop Nicholas wrote differently and spoke differently.

Probably in 1424 Chelčický wrote his final answer to Bishop Nicholas, the Replika proti Mikuláši Biskupci Táborskému, which put an end to his friendly but strained relations with the Táborites.

... I think it was three years ago that you were at Vodniany with the priest Lucas, and there you sent for me and asked me to tell you what I had heard about you since there were some that spoke well of you, and others ill... Then, after a long time, you sent for me again... I like the things you said to me ... and I asked you to write out for me your views...

In this *Reply* Chelčický refuted the latter's accusation that he extorted from him, under a false pretext, some of his writings. At this date (1424) Peter Chelčický knew much more about the issues involved in the Eucharist than when he wrote about the four essences (1421-2), and he admitted this candidly:

I did not ask for it (*i.e.* the Bishop's writing) by any ruse, because I knew then concerning those things (the Táborite doctrine of the Eucharist) – of which I am now writing – very little; in fact, I knew about them as much then as I do know now what the Pope is doing in Rome at this moment... I loved you (*i.e.* the Táborite priests) more than any other priests ... therefore I am more sorry for you than the others.

It is possible that the Bishop accused Chelčický of false intentions in order to play safe when, after General Žižka's death in 1424, Master John of Příbram, the Inquisitor of the Utraquists, began speeding up his purging of Táborite influences. This hypothesis becomes all the more plausible if we remember that later, after the bloody liquidation of the last Táborite remnants in politics, Bishop Nicholas was imprisoned on orders of King George in his own castle of Podiebrad in 1452, where he died seven years later.

The Estrangement from the Utraquists

In parting his ways with Nicholas, Peter put an end to his relations with the Táborite faction. But, even though abandoned by all his old friends, Chelčický did not remain alone; about this time (1425) he began to speak of "us" and "some of us." This was a faint echo of the birth of the nucleus out of which was later born the Unity of Brethren, the "Moravian" Church.

For a while, Chelčický was in good relations with the Utraquist Church and its controversial archbishop, John Rokycana. Many letters were exchanged between these two men. In another place we spoke of Rokycana's mediation between Chelčický and a group of young reformists. But Rokycana gradually became more and more what we might call a "high-church" man, with Romanist leanings. This in the end alienated him from Chelčický, who wrote a sharp polemical *Replika proti Rokycanovi* (A Reply to Archbishop Rokycana).

There followed other works, all of a polemical nature against the Utraquist doctrines and practices. Just as ten years before, his *Reply to Bishop Nicholas* signified a rupture with the Táborites, so now the *Reply to Archbishop Rokycana* symbolizes the severance with the Utraquists. Both *Replies* stand as milestones on the road of his development, which points away from the doctrinarian strife and sacerdotalism of the Hussite factions, and toward a life of more abundant Christian expression.

31

Peter Chelčický and His Life

Year	Chelčický's Life	Historic Events	King of Bohemia	Anti-popes	Popes
	Peter Záhorka born in Brezi, 1374-81	— Milíč of Kroměříž dies, 1374	Karel I 1346-1378		Gregory XI 1370-1378
1380			Václav IV 1378-1419	Clement VII 1378-1394	Urban VI 1378-1389
		— John Wyclif dies, 1384			
1390	Peter Chelčický born in Chelčice, 1390				Boniface IX 1389-1404
				Benedict XIII 1394-1423	
1400					
					Innocent VII / Gregory XII 1406-1415
1410				Alexander V / John XXIII 1410-1415	
		— John Hus burned, 1415			
	University Masters questioned about war, 1419				Martin V 1417-1431
1420	Spiritual Warfare, 1421	— Nicholas made Tábor bishop, 1420	Sigismund		
	Holy Church, conference with Nicholas, 1422				
	Three Estates, 1425	— Žižka dies, 1424	Hussite Wars 1420-1436	Clement VIII 1423-1429 / Benedict XIVa 1425-1429	
	Reply to Nicholas, 1421				
1430					
	Seven Sacraments, 1432	— Joan of Arc burned, 1431	Benedict XIVb 1430-1437		Eugene IV 1431-1447
	Reply to Rokycana, 1434	— Battle of Lipany, 1434			
			Sigismund / Albert 1437-1439		
1440	Net of Faith, 1440-43	— Donation of Constantine exposed as forgery, 1440	George of Podiebrad as regent for Ladislav I 1440-1453	Felix V 1439-1449	
	Divine Body, 1444				
	Postilla, 1443-46				
1450					Nicholas V 1447-1455
		— Bishop Nicholas imprisoned, 1452	Ladislav I 1453-1457		
		— Unitas Fratrum founded, 1457	George of Podiebrad 1458-1471		Callixtus III 1455-1458
1460	— Peter Chelčický dies, 1460	— Bishop Nicholas dies, 1459			Pius II 1458-1464

Chapter 5

Peter Chelčický, His Philosophy

When God commands a thing to be done against the customs or compact of any people, though it was never by them done heretofore, it is to be done.

– St. Augustine

This yearning for a life of more abundant Christian expression was incorporated in Chelčický's greatest work, the *Net of True Faith*, written sometime between the years 1440-1443, during the interregnum following the death of King Albrecht of Hapsburg. His whole philosophy of life and history is represented in this book. Its central theme is the relation of the Church and state, and the Christian's place in that relation. The thesis is presented in the form of an exposition of the story of the miraculous "inclusion of fishes" according to Luke's narrative (5:4-11). As far as we know, this is a unique interpretation of the gospel story; in most medieval treatises, learned men and theologians wasted themselves in fanciful trivialities. But Chelčický, starting with his allegory and bringing out its ethical, political, and economic implications goes far beyond these stereotyped commentaries. In reading his interpretation of the story we realize that rarely have any advocates … whether ancient or modern, worked out its implications with such rigorous logic, such thoroughgoing consistency, and such singleness of aim, as Peter Chelčický had done.

In his allegory, the net becomes the symbol of the Christian religion; in the net there is a multitude of fish caught by the apostles who are aided by Jesus. They represent the Christians. The loving will of God offers to men His net of faith in Jesus Christ and with it his salvation. And so there comes down into the sea of human bondage, sin, and misery a veritable

34

symbol of the divine *agapé*, the net of faith, to do its work of redemption. But the net became greatly torn

when two great whales had entered it, that is, the Supreme Priest wielding royal power and honor superior to the Emperor, and the second whale being the Emperor who, with his rule and offices, smuggled pagan power and violence beneath the skin of faith. And when these two monstrous whales began to turn about in the net, they rent it to such an extent that very little of it has remained intact. From these two whales, so destructive of Peter's net, there were spawned many scheming schools by which that net is also so greatly torn that nothing but tatters and false names remain...

A Miniature Drawing from the Book *Hortus Deliciarum*

The nearest resemblance to Chelčický's net of faith in treatment and motif that we could find is contained in the noted *Hortus deliciarum* of the Abbess Herrade of Landsberg which reproduced pictorially an idea founded on the Book of Job (41:1ff), and of which Mâle traces the seminal thought back to St. Jerome in the 5th century, and thence down through St. Gregory the Great, St. Odo of Cluny, and Bruno of Asti, to Honorius d'Autun who thus described the symbolism:

36

Leviathan the monster swims in the sea of the world, *i.e.* Satan. God has thrown the line into that sea. The cord of that line is the human genealogy of Christ; the hook is the divinity of Christ; the bait is his humanity. Attracted by the scent of his flesh, Leviathan wants to snap him, but the hook tears apart his jaw.

The Donation of Constantine

The background for Chelčický's allegory is his belief in the so-called Donation of Constantine, a belief, by the way, based on the authority of John Hus, and probably also on the Waldensian version of the Donation.

There was drawn up, presumably in the papal chancellery during the third quarter of the eighth century, a forged document alleged to be a donation of the Emperor Constantine to Pope Sylvester I. This document relates that when the pagan Constantine was healed of leprosy, by the pope, he professed Christianity. In gratitude he decided to vacate Rome, removing the imperial capital to Constantinople. As his legacy to Sylvester he left

... our imperial Lateran palace, ... likewise all provinces, places and districts of the City of Rome ... and bequeathing them to the power and sway of him and the pontiffs, his successors, we do ... determine and decree that the same be placed at his disposal, and do lawfully grant it as a permanent possession to the exalted Holy Roman Church ... The Sacred See of Blessed Peter shall be gloriously exalted above our empire and earthly throne ... And the pontiff who for the time being presides over the most holy Roman Church shall be ruler as well over the four principal sees, Antioch, Alexandria, Constantinople, and Jerusalem...

The papal theocracy based its whole legal justification on the imposing Petrine theory combined with the forged Pseudo-Isidorian Decretals, of which the *Donatio Constantini* is just one document. All men of the Middle Ages believed in this donation, and so did Peter Chelčický. It was often quoted by popes and papal partisans in their subsequent struggles for temporal power. For seven hundred years it was believed to be authentic, even though there were men who wished it were a forgery, which Nicholas of Cusa had suspected, but the honor of discovering their

37

falsehood was left to Lorenzo Valla, the famous Italian humanist, who showed in a scathing work of 1440, *De falso credita et emendita Constantini donatione declamatio*, that its Latin could not possibly have been written in the fourth century. Be it as it may, the fact remains that by the Edict of Milan Constantine raised Christianity to equality with the public pagan cults; the final act was the seizure of the power of the state and the banning of other competing cults.

By utilizing the mechanism of the State, the Church lived through the ruin of the State and lived to tell the tale. That act betrayed the spirit of Jesus and established the reign of Christ...

Constantine insisted upon unity within the Church and hence was drawn into the problems of sectarian strife. In this sphere he undertook to uphold the opinion of the majority of bishops and exercised the right to summon and preside over councils and to validate and enforce their decisions. This exercise of imperial authority in religious matters was the initial step in the development of caesaro-papism.

Frontispiece Illustration of the 1521 Edition of The Net of Faith

Printed in the Monastery of Vilémov

(The net is held by four apostles and in the net are the righteous Christians. One sinner is falling overboard and another is escaping through a big hole in the torn net. Below, protruding from the open jaw of an infernal leviathan, the devil is roping in the pope, the emperor, the learned doctors, and other sinners.)

Chelčický did not possess the phenomenal historic knowledge of Lorenzo Valla, and he never heard of the latter's discoveries. He did not doubt the authenticity of the Donation but he attacked its juridical validity on ethical and Biblical grounds. It is a strange coincidence that both books, *The Net of Faith* and the *Declamatio de Donatione* should have been published almost simultaneously. Each of these books, one written in humanist Italy, and the other in "heretical" Bohemia, represented a mighty blow at ecclesiastical imperialism and falsehood.

Chelčický's historic presupposition was wrong but his ultimate analysis of the secularization of the Church and its identification with the temporal power was correct. Mythologically, the Donation presents a profound truth. It was when the Donation took place, according to Chelčický, that the "two great whales" – the Emperor and the Pope – entered the net of faith, "rending it in many places." Declaring the law of God to be the sole rule of faith and life, he postulated the abolition of all church institutions not compatible with this law and introduced by man, as well as the abrogation of all secular institutions, social orders, and state orders inconsistent with Christ's law of love.

The State

Chelčický antedates Kropotkin by several centuries when he writes that the state is based on violence, plunder, and proud individualism. But where Kropotkin speaks in terms of economics, Chelčický speaks with prophetic earnestness in terms of a theocentric history. As he sees it, Gideon, the "faithful Jew" of the Old Testament, answered his followers with true divine sanction when he refused the crown they had come to offer to him:

I will not rule over you, nor shall my sons rule over you, since the Lord God rules over you!

The state has its origin in man's pride and rebellion against God. Just as the Jews rejected the law of God by inviting Saul to rule over them, so the Christians later on rejected God by accepting the Donation of Constantine. And having its origin in sin, the state has become a tool of punishment. This is well illustrated in the records of King Solomon's rule that, in all the glory of his wisdom, brought terrible sufferings upon his people.

The state's existence may be justifiable as a "necessary evil" only for the pagans among whom it works "as a plaster on an abscess" since, if they had "no prince with a sword in his hands," there would be no justice, but a war of all people against all, and depravity and violence would be the general rule. However, the heathens know not the teachings of Christ who tells us to love our neighbor and to do good to those who persecute us. And Christians? They must abstain from all violence:

Our faith obliges us to bind wounds, not to make blood run...

Therefore, a Christian state is a contradiction in terms. For it is in the nature of the state to rule by coercion and force. However, the rule of Christ is perfect, and therefore it never uses compulsion... The virtue that he expects from every Christian ... springs from a good and free will; originating in freedom, it has the responsibility of choice, to choose either the best or the worst.

A Christian cannot rule, for God is the only ruler. A secular ruler is bound, by virtue of his sovereignty, to use violence and other non-Christian methods. If he should, perchance, become a Christian, his only means of ruling would then be persuasion, that is, preaching:

... for otherwise, by forcing Christians, he will not succeed. But if a king ... preaches, he is not a king any more, he becomes a priest. As a king he should be able to do naught but hang all evil men. For no king, not even the best one, could succeed in rehabilitating an evil people except by the law of Christ.

In this teaching, Chelčický comes very close to the Gelasian doctrine of the two powers. Furthermore, says he, sovereignty goes always hand in hand with aggressiveness and imperialism. It is in the nature of all rulers to use un-Christian means for their ends of aggrandizement:

They try to embrace as much of the earth as they are able, using every means and every ruse of violence to get hold of the territory of the weaker; sometimes by money, and at other times by inheritance, but always desiring to rule and to extend their realm as far as they can.

That is why no Christian can have any part in any government. He is good because it is God's will and not because the state requires it. His ethic is therefore superior to that of non-Christians who abide only by a legal goodness. For the same reason, no Christian can exercise authority over another Christian. This fundamental postulate underlies all of Chelčický's philosophy. It carries with it many implications: a Christian cannot tax another Christian – however, if Christians live in a non-Christian state, they ought to pay their taxes for the sake of public peace. A Christian may not perform military service for that means imposition of a coercive burden on other Christians.

Men are governed not so much by the tyrants they fear as by the institutions they love; and what is, therefore, more worth loving than the "sweet rule of Christ?" In the long run love – not fear, coercion, and hatred – will prevail:

O how small and barren is the dominion of pagan kings compared with the dominion of Christ! The temporal power heaps burdens and sufferings upon its subjects instead of freedom and consolation. And yet, the Kingdom of Christ is so powerful and perfect that, if the whole world wanted him for king, it would have peace, and all things would work together for good. And there would be no need of temporal rulers, for all and sundry would stand by grace and truth. The need of kings arises, indeed, because of sins and sinners.

42

To him who obeys God the state becomes a superfluity, for the fullness of the law is love:

Judge for yourself, how can state authority approach those who are bound by the divine commandment not to resist evil in times of adversity, but to offer the other cheek when the one is struck, to leave revenge to God and not to return evil for evil…?

Chelčický does not argue against any state as such, but against the abuse that such a center of power and violence is given a Christian name and justification. While on earth, the Christians are a true colony of heaven and the laws of heaven are undefiled by compulsion. These laws are different from the "earthly" laws in that they never enforce obedience man has to turn away from his evil ways by his own volition; and there are always two alternatives before man:

The Lord Jesus calls us to the best good, the devil and the world call us to the worst evil. Therefore, choose joy or choose hell. The choice of either of these ways is in your hands.

In the fourteenth chapter, one of the most important chapters of the whole book, Chelčický sums up in eloquent words the core of his conviction that "Christ's commandment of love could make one multitude out of a thousand worlds, one heart, and one soul… It will lead man into the fullest life, it will make him most precious to God, and man will become a gain to man!"

The Church

God is the end; love is the means. That is the rule of Christ's kingdom whose earthly image is the Church. Christ is the true head of the Church, "the beginning of his kingdom is at the end of men's sins" and his law is love.

This law is sufficient of itself and adequate for a redeeming administration of God's people.

It is an apotheosis of free will and it functions only when man responds through personal discipline to the divine *agapé*. The Church comprises all righteous Christians gathered in the Net of Faith by the apostles. As long as Christ was the sole ruler of the apostolic Church – that is, for the first three hundred years, it was perfect. But when Pope Sylvester accepted the Donation of Constantine the net of faith became badly torn. And when he allied the Church with secular power he "mixed poison with Christ's gospel." Since then, the social utility of the priestly Church has been to invoke divine sanctions in defense of the status quo, however bad.

Indeed, the Church of Rome rather likes a wicked king, for this man ... will fight for her better than a humble Christian.

In order to increase the power of the Church, the Pope arrogated to himself all prerogatives of Christ,and this he manages lucratively, initiating a pilgrimage to Rome from all countries ... and proclaiming to all pilgrims forgiveness of all sins...

Through participation in power politics, by condoning wars and even by issuing war bonds for their prosecution, the Church of Rome lost its spiritual heritage. Only those who obey Christ are members of the true Church. The true Church was not to be found even among the Hussites, those "raging locusts."

Chelčický gave considerable thought and attention to one of the most important and spectacular events of Christendom in his age, the Council of Basel. Out of ninety-five chapters of his *Net of Faith* he devoted a full fifteen chapters to the Basel proceedings. Needless to say, he was very disappointed in the display of power and ecclesiastical hypocrisy so manifest at Basel. He was scandalized at the Pharisaic ratiocinations proffered by high church dignitaries in the name of Christian truth. The Council may have repeatedly pronounced that the Holy Spirit was presiding over it, but Chelčický saw nothing in it but the work of the devil himself:

Let him who is humble and meek come and behold the vainglorious haughtiness! For a congregation of fornicators has entered into a covenant with the Holy Spirit and the Holy Spirit reigns over them who are an assembly of harlots, assassins of righteous men, and transgressors of all commandments of God... The devil, who dwells among us under a shadow as it were, has a rich accoutrement indeed. And who shall unveil his face, which he hides by the shadow of the Holy Spirit?

He took to task especially the Papal Auditor Juan Palomar, one of the chief opponents of the Hussite position, and the Parisian professor of theology Giles Charlier, who had several public disputations with the Táborite Bishop Nicholas of Pelhřimov. In reading those pages of *The Net of Faith* that deal with the Council of Basel we cannot but be impressed by Chelčický' s deep shock and holy wrath at the double ethic of men who were supposed to represent western Christendom. And we realize more clearly the urgent necessity of Reformation. With all the faults that Chelčický saw in Hussitism it still was a clean current in the midst of the stagnant waters of medieval Christianity. Its representatives alone insisted on the removal of the several hundred prostitutes from Basel during the council session. And it was Giles Charlier who took upon himself the task of defending the presence of prostitution in Basel. In its defense he used scriptural references as well as such authorities as St. Jerome and St. Augustine.

The old saints, in their concern for the well-being of the communities, provided them with legality concerning harlots, so that a town, suffering from lustfulness, might be relieved of it by communal prostitutes. This the Master Aegidius confirms with the help of Church Doctors!

The learned men of Basel and the Church doctors may know a great deal, said Chelčický, but they know nothing about a Christian life "lived in perfection and in accordance with the law of God."

He little respected the Church doctors and saints used by the Romanists to bolster up their patristic edifice of power. Albertus Magnus, the most respected medieval authority of ecclesiastical learning, he called "that loudly howling Albertus," and he was not much more flattering to St. Augustine to whom he often referred to as "that pillar standing in Rome." He felt that it was St. Augustine who was the most responsible for

45

providing the Roman Church with a theology of ecclesiastical imperialism:

That great pillar of the Church of Rome which supports her strongly that she may not fall, gave to the gospel the spirit of a sharp sword...

But the greatest sin the Church has committed is her alliance with the state and with the secular methods of power, institutionalism, and coercion.

The Church of Rome has allied herself with the state, and now they both drink together the blood of Christ, one from a chalice, and the other from the ground where it was spilled by the sword.

The Christians have fallen short of the ideal and the only remedy is to obey the Inner Light that comes of the grace of God.

Christian Socialism and Communism

The founder of the German Reformation has written somewhere that man could *change* but that only God could *better.* But oddly Luther – the son of a peasant – failed to explain why God worked so exclusively on the side of the ruling classes. Chelčický – the son of a nobleman, if the Záhorka theory proves correct – insisted that the devil rather preferred working with the ruling noblemen and churchmen!

...The pagans do not have ... to contend with so many lords and useless clergymen who all hold great dominions... Yes, they do not bear their sword in vain, they rob and oppress the poor working people.

The nobility and the priesthood have "alienated the people from God." Naturally, Chelčický did not accept Wyclif's division of men into three estates (noblemen, priests, and the working people). Such division, said he, amounts to an enforced grouping of men into the following professions:

46

The estate of the ruling class which conducts defensive warfare, kills, burns, and hangs; the estate of the common and higher priests who pray; and the estate of the common peasants who must slave and feed the two upper-class insatiable Baals.

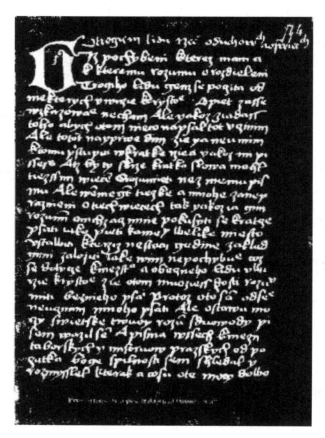

The First Page of the Manuscript *About the Three Estates*
by Peter Chelčický
(This document is preserved in the Library of the Metropolitan
Chapter of Prague, in the Codex "D.32" on folios marked 74a-103a.
It may represent Chelčický's own handwriting.)

This division is contrary to the law of Christ and only leads to further evils.

Today authority is a sweet affair to the king opulent with fat and licentious in living … to whom the word "peasant" is repugnant… But woe unto him when he shall meet the words of God face to face! Then his violences shall be met with great discomforts to his well-being, and he shall cry blind, "Alas! Woe is me! Why has my mother ever begotten me into this world!"

To divide Christendom into classes is tantamount to dividing the body of Christ.

Naturally, this order is agreeable to the first two classes who loaf, gorge, and dissipate themselves. And the burden for this living is shoved onto the shoulders of the third class which has to pay in suffering for the pleasures of the other two guzzlers – and there are so many of them!

There are many eloquent passages that show that Chelčický was far ahead of his time with his strong social consciousness:

And if you who are heavy and round with fat object saying, "Our fathers have bought these people and those manors for our inheritance," then, indeed, they made an evil business and an expensive bargain! For who has the right to buy people, to enslave them, and to treat them with indignities as if they were cattle? … You prefer dogs to people whom you cuss, despise, beat, from whom you extort taxes, and for whom you forge fetters … while at the same time you will say to your dog, "Setter, come here and lie down on the pillow." Those people were God's before you bought them!

Wyclif's sanction of the old threefold division only perpetuates the old evil that Christ came to abolish. He came to make men free:

(He) bought this people to himself – not with silver and gold – but with his own precious blood and terrible suffering… The heavenly Lord redeems and buys the people for his inheritance. And the earthly lord buys them in order to (enslave them).

God's wrath will terribly punish the ruling upper class that abetted social exploitation:

Look, you fat one, what a sodomitic life you have prepared for your people! What will you say on the Day of Judgment when the Lord will seat Himself on the judgment throne, and when all injustices committed against this people – yes, the very people which He Himself bought with His blood – will be arraigned against you? And He will say to you, "As you did it to one of the least of these my brethren, you did it to me. Go to hell!" And no high titles, no archives, no records, no documents with seals … will save you from perdition.

Chelčický's socialism is not a dialectic materialism; to speak figuratively, he stands on firm Biblical ground and examines his contemporary society with a strong searchlight of Christ's ethic. What he finds is devastating, and his conclusions are more radical than those of Marx or Lenin. Christian faith is dead unless it can show fruits of its existence.

For faith apart from works is dead, useless, and devilish; real faith is alive, useful, and Christian.

His communism is thoroughly Christian, springing from a theocentric view of life:

The earth is the Lord's and its fullness, that is, its mountains and valleys and all regions… Who is not God's, has no right to possess or to hold anything that belongs to God, unless he has taken possession of it illegally and by violence. Thus, contrary to the divine law, our fathers bought and established illegal claims for us … and this is our natural heritage: poverty, shame, and death… But God shall regard all these unlawful property holders as traitors of the Kingdom of God.

True followers of Christ obey the commandments of God, love their neighbors as themselves, and cannot therefore take part in any unjust "manner of pagan rulership."

Luther weakened the foundation of the Church by strengthening the fortifications of the state; Chelčický proclaimed that both the Church and the State were built on quicksand, and that all earnest Christians must build a new society on the firm foundation of "Christ's law of love."

Pacifism

"If a murder is committed privately it is a crime, but if it happens with state authority, courage is the name for it." Chelčický echoed these words of Cyprian with the whole being of his personality. Basing his conviction on Christ's teaching he fully adopted the position of the early Church Fathers and in many ways anticipated Tolstoy and Gandhi in trying to seek the source of war.

"The sword separates the Christian from God," he wrote in *The Net of Faith*. In the sight of God, war is always murder. What is the beginning of wars?

Their root is in intemperate self-love and an immoderate affection for temporal possessions. And these conflicts are brought into this world because men do not trust the Son of God enough to abide by his commandments.

Covetousness and lust for power are the cause of every war. Cain was surfeited with pride of possessions; for this reason he was the first to fortify a city, since it is inevitable that possessors always have to think of aggressors.

The lords try to embrace as much of the earth as they are able, using every means and every ruse or violence to get hold of the territory of the weaker, sometimes by money and at other times by inheritance, but always desiring to rule and to extend their realm as far as they can.

"Death sits in the shadow of authority" which exercises its power contrary to Christ's will and a Christian has a duty to resist it. An arrogant state authority is a trap for good Christians; it compels its subjects to go and do every evil it can think of Christ's death established a covenant relationship between man and God that outlawed war forever. Military service and conscription are "compulsory sins" and to obey the call issued either by the state or the Church is tantamount to honoring sin and the devil. The conscripted men run to war doing to their neighbors that which God has forbidden and which would not be tolerated at home. The commandment of God says, "So whatever you wish that men would do to you, do so to them." But he who goes to war does evil to them of whom he would wish that they do good to him; and what he would be loath doing at home, that he gladly does obeying the orders of his lords.

The true followers of Jesus would rather be martyrs than be accomplices in war:

They would refuse to storm the walls, to run like cattle, to destroy, to murder and to rob; instead, they would rather perish under the sword than to do these things so revolting to the law of God.

True Christians must obey their authorities passively and pay their taxes, but active participation is incompatible with Christian virtues.

Man is possessed by the possessions he has. A Christian should not be a slave of material things.

A pagan fights to protect his rights and his property in court or in field; a Christian conducts his life with love, patiently enduring injustice, as he will be rewarded by an eternal gain.

A Christian must abstain therefore from courts and lawsuits. And it goes without saying that capital punishment contradicts the law of love. The priests who support the state authority in its "right" to conduct wars and enforce justice by capital punishment are making God as having two mouths, with one saying, "you shall not kill," and with the other, you shall kill.

51

God is the sovereign, the Pantokrator, and all human sovereignties, states, and possessions are as nothing in His eyes:

Who becomes acquainted with the law of God cannot create nor recognize nor obey any other law, for no other law is right.

God is love.

Chelčický's Style

Peter Chelčický's *Net of Faith* does not read as easily as the *Praise of Folly* by Erasmus of Rotterdam; it is the product of a man who did not have a formal education that the other absorbed in abundance. We often notice at the beginning of chapters that he meets difficulty in going into the *medias res*; he is redundant, at times cumbersome, but once he warms up to his subject, he can write passages of rare beauty and spiritual insight. He is not afraid of using homespun turns of speech or afraid of calling a spade a spade.

His life on the farm in Chelčice is reflected in many illustrations taken from the agricultural environment:

Many a king does not know the King of Heaven, but he still is like a plough in the hands of the plowman.

This world that seeks God on the surface is like a goat gnawing the outer bark of a willow; the power and aliveness of faith is hidden from it.

(The Pope) was grafted by the Emperor onto the tree of pagan rule in order to enjoy a most exalted priesthood, and everything stemming from the grafting of this tree is supposed to be more worthy of respect.

Chelčický is no introvert when writing; especially when carried away by his righteous indignation of social injustices or ecclesiastical stupidity and hypocrisy; he does not mince his words and often uses harsh expressions:

(The Pope) seldom celebrates mass, never preaches, and never works; that is, the only work which he instituted for himself is the blessing of those whom he loves and the excommunication of those he does not love. And so he lies in luxuries and gorges himself like a hog wallowing in a sty.

And all this (decadence) has been smuggled into faith with the pagan rule like an evil smelling corpse, to the great defilement of faith...

The Net of Faith is full of vivid illustrations of the medieval life and is most descriptive, especially in the second volume. That section, from the literary point of view more interesting in many respects, is not included in this thesis because it is an elaboration of the main philosophy presented in Book One.

In the Czech original, *The Net of Faith* represents a gem of medieval Bohemian literature, excelling in originality of style, purity of expression untouched by foreign affectations, masculine straightforwardness, and occasional tenderness that brings him very close to an authentic mystic expression:

"If any man wants to come after me, let him deny himself and take up his cross and follow me." And if your physical will does not want it and rebels against it, compel it yourself. You yourself must rebel against your unwilling will and follow reason. Deny yourself; cling to God through grace, fulfilling His good will by emptying your own ill-will, for the love of God your Lord!

Throughout the book Brother Peter of Chelčice speaks to us with a great urgency; let us listen to him, for the Burden of the Lord is upon him. "Woe unto those who are at ease in Rome and in Prague," cries the Amos of Bohemia; yet, throughout his message there is a warm undertone of ever-present Divine love. It is this undertone that gives *The Net of Faith* its true grandeur and a relevance for our own "misguided and distraught times:"

Our faith obliges us to bind wounds, not to make blood run.

AMEN

PART II

TRANSLATION OF
THE NET OF FAITH,
BOOK ONE:

THE CORRUPTION OF THE CHURCH, CAUSED BY ITS FUSION AND CONFUSION WITH TEMPORAL POWER

A Statue of Peter Chelčický by Professor Jan Straka of Prague

Foreword

Prefaced to the Vilémov Edition of 1521

by Chval Dubánek

This book is very needful for these misguided and distraught times. It received the name or title of *The Net of Faith* which was written (and) composed by a man, honest, noble and holy in the hope of God, richly endowed for this task by the bounty of our Lord and filled with the wisdom of the Holy Spirit; and his name is Peter of Chelčice. This man was shining with the inward gifts of God in the days of Master Rokycana, and was well known to the master since he often abided in his presence. The said Peter wrote many divers and most useful and necessary books about the Law of our Lord, leaving them to the Holy Church in order to aid her in her struggle against the Anti-Christ and his snares.

And so, whoever you may be who shall often read in these books and look into them, you will have to admit that it pleased Almighty God our Lord not to forget our forefathers but, on the contrary, to pour out His Holy Spirit upon them so that, being able to understand the Scriptures of the Holy Law according to the spirit of Jesus Christ, they might share with others of future generations the remembrance of these gifts that were given into their trust.

If the books of this man Peter of Chelčice have not frequently seen light until recently, the cause is to be sought nowhere else but in the priesthood of the Pope of the Anti-Christ; which priesthood – with many of its number living disreputably and ignobly – has not ceased and even today is not desisting from defaming before the general public the books of this excellent man by calling them schismatic and heretical, for no other reason except that (the reading of them) shrinks their benefice, reduces the offerings in their plates, and scares them away from their rich soup. For he said about them that they wasted the substance of the Law of God with uttonous living behind rich tables and that they drowned the light of exemplary living with costly and rare wines.

It is these very priests who, flushed with anger against Peter, condemn him acrimoniously as a heretic. But good and honest priests do love him and make use of his books.

The Almighty Lord and most gracious God does not withhold His gifts from those who seek Him; it pleases Him to award them from the bountiful store of His inspiration, so that they might put aside all threats of the Antichrist and his harmless intimidations and, getting hold of the truth written down in these books inspired by the Spirit, love and study it as a gift of our Lord God Almighty for these latter times and days of the Antichrist.

Numerous men of almost all estates – the estate of Christ's priests, the estate of the Lords and the estate of the Knights, the estate of the Burghers as well as of many learned and common people – all of them cherish, accept, and honor the truths of these books and other writings of Peter Chelčický; and they do not slight him because he is a layman, not learned in the Latin tongue. For though he was not a master of the seven arts, he certainly was a practitioner of the eight beatitudes and of all the divine commandments, and was therefore a real Czech doctor, well versed in the Law of the Lord without aberration from the truth. In him was fulfilled the word of the prophet saying, "Blessed is the man whom you chasten, and teach of your law, O Lord," and in another Psalm,

"O God, you have taught me from my youth and hitherto have I declared your wondrous works. Yes, even to old age and gray hairs, do not forsake me, O God."

And even our Lord Jesus says in the Gospel of Saint John,

"All men will be taught by God. Everyone that listens to the Father and has learned from him will come to me."

57

O how happy and blessed are the disciples who are taught in such a way by the Lord God in the school of the Holy Spirit, the best of teachers, who learn the law of the Lord and the sense and meaning of Christ! They and those like them are coming to the Lord and they are truly the disciples of the Lord, following their Lord Jesus in humility and meekness, as he himself has expressed it. Rejoicing in the Holy Spirit he said,

"I praise you, Father, Lord of heaven and earth, that you have hidden these things from the wise and prudent, and have revealed them to babes. Yes, I thank you, Father, for so it seemed good in your sight."

This was fulfilled in the holy prophets, in the son of God the Highest, our Lord Jesus, in the holy Apostles chosen from among the whole world, that is, chosen not only from among those learned in human wisdom, in logic, and in pagan art, but also from among the poor orders, from fishers' craft, from the common people. You may find proof to this in the Acts of the Apostles:

"Now, when they saw the boldness of Peter and John, and perceived that they were uneducated, common men, they wondered."

That is, they were surprised to find such a power in the teaching of the Lord and such miracles which the Lord God performed through them; for the knowledge of God is vast and far above the knowledge of man, just as the heavens are higher than the earth. And the knowledge of God makes man meek and humble, while the wisdom of man puffs up and gives itself air through pride. Therefore, this excellent man Peter Chelčický, the chosen vessel of the Lord, being endowed with many gifts through the grace of God and having learned in the highest school of the Holy Spirit, brings forth old and new things out of the treasures of the Lord, writing these most useful and necessary books for everyone and all men of all estates.

And Peter writes about every one of the estates, revealing their corrupting evils. He begins with the highest estates: the estates of the emperors, kings, dukes, lords, knights, burghers, and guilds, as well as those of the common people, not forgetting to rebuke even the peasants for their disorders. But he writes especially and above everything else against the so-called spiritual estates: the popes, the cardinals, the bishops, the archbishops, the abbots, and the orders of monks and mendicant friars, as well as the deacons and pastors, the chaplains, and all this debauched, ignoble, haughty, avaricious, lascivious, parsimonious, beery generation of clergy, stubbornly steeped in all mortal sins and heresies. He writes not, however, against honest, honorable, and faithful priests. But he courageously attacks and speaks against papal inventions, uncertain human prevarications, and all other insincerities, for all these above named people do not cease from continually tearing the apostolic net until almost nothing is left but rags and tatters and confused knots.

The first part of the book consists in disclosing the manner in which such a terrible confusion has come upon the Holy Church. It also shows that whoever would like to dig down to the real ground and true foundation, which is Jesus Christ, would have to remove and cart out to the edge of town a lot of debris consisting of prevarications wriggled into the Holy Church by men.

The second part of the book consists in revealing how the estates and castes and all the multiform teachings and un-Christian religions have originated. All these estates and divisions are a great obstacle in the way to the knowledge of faith in Jesus the Lord, for they have put on the garb of the spirit of pride and haughtiness, resisting as much as they can our humble and poor Lord Jesus.

CHAPTER 1

THE MIRACULOUS FISHING

Now when Jesus had ceased speaking, he said to Simon Peter, "Push out into the deep and let down your nets for a haul." And Simon answering said, "Master, we tolled all night and caught nothing. Nevertheless, at your word I will let down the net." And when they had done this, they enclosed such a great shoal of fish that their net began to break.

59

These words written in the Gospel are the foundation of those matters that ought to be profitably taught, to some for usefulness, to others for irritation, provocation, ill will, and disfavor. In this respect, however, we will, with God's help, deal with nothing else but that we of the latter day desire to see the first things, and to take hold of them, if He will let us do so. For the worst time has come, the time of storm, the time of crying and moaning, the time of all sorts of deception, which makes it possible that every one to the last man be deceived by signs and miracles performed by false Christs. And none would be able to withstand them were it not that God has shortened these times for His chosen people.

Thus we of the latter day are like after the burning out of a house which has fallen down making a pile of ruins; here and there we see by some signs that there stood a chamber before — but everything fell onto the foundation (which, buried,) is grown over by a forest where animals graze and dwell. Who will then find the buried foundation of the burned house that is in ruins and which is deeply covered (with debris) and the top of which has long since been overgrown by defiant weeds?

The whole matter of finding the true foundation is made all the more difficult because these defiant weeds which have sprung upon it are called the true foundation by many; they, pulling to themselves the growth on top of the house ruins, declare, "This is the foundation and the way, all should follow it." And with many of them we see that their new foundation sinks into soft ground, the floor settling at different levels. This shows the difficulty of finding the true foundation...

There are many who would like to dig in order to find the original foundation, in the like manner as Nehemiah, Zerubbabel, and the prophets have done, when, after seventy years of their Babylonian captivity, they returned and built the Temple of the Lord which had been burned down by the Edomites. And they had a great difficulty in rebuilding the city and the Temple on the charred ruins. Now there are also spiritual ruins long ago covered up (by weeds); these, too, shall be mended and rebuilt, and for this no one can give a true foundation save Jesus Christ from whom many have run away to other gods, building themselves new foundations, denying and covering up Jesus Christ, the Son of God, by a (layer of) falsehood.

CHAPTER 2

INTERPRETATION OF THE MIRACULOUS FISHING

We have before us the words of the Gospel about which we wish to speak; we would like especially to comment on these three points:

> ▶ Simon Peter says, "Master, we worked all night and caught nothing."
> ▶ "Nevertheless, at your word I will let down the net."
> ▶ And when they had done this, they enclosed such a great shoal of fish that their nets began to break.

Having written out these words, let us look at their spiritual meaning, especially since these words have a different connotation spiritually than (what they imply) physically.

The wearisome but fruitless fishing, an activity at which Peter spent a whole night wading in the water without catching anything, is a symbol and an example of the spiritual night in which all human effort is without result; no one can catch any heavenly reward. It is thus with profit that we are told:

The night is far-gone; the day is at hand. Let us then cast off the works of darkness and put on the armor of light; let us conduct ourselves becomingly as in the day.

The night is pagan ignorance and Jewish blindness which passed away when Christ, the Son of God, the True Light, came into the world in order to illumine those who lived in the shadow of death.

61

Therefore, let us look at the meaning and practicability of the aforesaid quotation. First of all, during a night of spiritual blindness, any human work is without result for those who have not attained to the light of Christ, a light brighter than day. And here we touch upon the most important part to which a Christian ought to pay his first attention. For every human generation is preoccupied with difficult enterprises, expecting early returns from them, and many even hoping for external gains, yet they labor at night only. Therefore wise men, who believe that now is the time for work deserving eternal joys, ought always to watch that their labor be not done during the night of ignorance and blindness – for all such effort is in vain. And one shall recognize the evil and uselessness of such vain deeds when one will move to the other world with empty hands. What can then such a person expect when it is said, "What shall I do? I cannot dig, and I am ashamed to beg." For there a rich man cannot have a single drop of water nor beg a single crumb. What can there be worse than to fall into an eternity of poverty with empty hands?

Such things are bound to occur to lazy people who waste their useful time because of their sluggishness; they did not want to work in summer, therefore they shall beg in winter, and nothing shall be given to them. And the others are bound to obtain eternal poverty with empty hands; we have already said of them that although they work much expecting heavenly reward for it, they shall not catch that which they hope to fish out, because they live in a night of sin and blindness. Therefore the foremost necessity of a careful servant is to insist that, when he works, the work be done in daylight.

Enough has been said about the unsuccessful fishing and the working at night. Saint Peter's speech is a sufficient answer when he said, "Nevertheless, at your word I will let down the net." It is here that the power of Christ's words is demonstrated because, what night could not have, His words have multiplied into abundance. For His words are so perfect and so powerful that not only those things which are made can become useful, but even those which are not made; this is in accordance with the Scripture which says:

By the word of the Lord the heavens were made, and by the breath of his mouth their entire host. Let all the earth fear the Lord; let all the inhabitants of the world stand in awe of him. For he spoke and it was! He commanded and it stood fast!

These words speak for themselves, demonstrating their power to command such happenings on earth and to introduce the laws of the heavens with their (manifold) fullness. That is why the writer of this passage says, "Let all the earth fear the Lord, and let all the inhabitants of the world stand in awe of him." If He can command all the heavens and the world in its entire beauty and perfection, how much more can he give orders to you, earthen people, who are like mosquitoes before him, like drops of water running spilled on the ground!

Perhaps (you think) the words of Jesus are not so powerful. Saint Paul says about the power of His words, Who being the brightness of his glory, and the express image of his person, and upholding all things by the word of his power...

He upholds all things, and creates those that were not. For through Him the world was made; His words are full of power. It is with regard to this strange power that Saint Peter says, "Nevertheless, at your word I will let down the net." After working all night without success Peter thinks that, spreading the net at the command of His word, he shall enclose many fishes. Here is the foundation on which the thoughts of the wise men should rest, namely, that only in the words of Christ are the works good and sufficient for salvation. For only His words are able to bring about good acts, and to empower them with validity and usefulness.

Secondly, His words are sufficient to the establishment of good acts since His words are a light in themselves, in accordance with the Scripture which says, "Your word is a lamp to my feet, O Lord God." That is, wherever I should go in the light of your word, I shall see, even though standing in the midst of darkness; I shall be able to direct my feet in such a way as not to fall and not to walk astray. And the light of God's word shows not only a path to good works, but it also reveals by what means man ought to accomplish his good works, in order to be glorified with

63

them. For who fights in battle shall not be crowned except he fight a good fight.

Thirdly, His words are sufficient to the establishment of good works because God loves and likes nothing except that which He chooses and wills to love. Therefore He loves nothing except that which He orders, commands, and teaches. Therefore He Himself found first in His own person those things He loves. These he desires and commands, and to them He gives His words, so that they, doing His will, may fulfill it. And it is imperative not only to fulfill His will, but also to find out – and we know this from His words – in what ways and by what means this will is to be fulfilled. And if, perchance, they departed in the least from His will, by the understanding of His words they would be made to know that they had succumbed to mortal sin.

That is why the word of God is good to the perception and fulfillment of His will. Thus, no matter what acts of great holiness man performs, they are not fulfilling and pleasing the Will of God if they do not spring from the truth of Christ's words. For there is not one man in all mankind who has an insight into God's counsel, there is not one (in the position) to ask about good deeds and to show to people a better way than the one which God has found in Himself, and which He has chosen; and that way He has published in the words of His commandments which are known to all who want to do His will and to find His grace. If they disdain His words, they shall draw upon themselves His wrath and carry it eternally with rebellious devils. This is the implication of faith to man.

In this sense the reply of Peter is to be understood when he says, "Nevertheless, at your word I will let down the net." He gives us a lesson of the true benefit of pursuing good works; we should not try to let down the nets for spiritual results except in obeying the words of Christ. Otherwise the work will be in vain. Our present world is full of such vain works, because it acts in accordance with ancient fancies and respectable renowned hypocrites; it looks to them for salvation and everyone seeks God on his own terms, as he likes and when he likes and where he likes, not giving much heed to whether God likes it or not.

The third implication of the story is this: "And when they had done this they enclosed such a great shoal of fish that their net began to break." These words portray the physical miracle (resulting) from the power of Christ's words. Through (these words) they caught so many fish that Peter's net began to break. These external physical manifestations can throw light on other spiritual realities: on Peter's spiritual 'fishing,' on his spiritual nets, and on spiritual spreading of the net. For it is apparent in this reading as well as in other passages that our Lord Jesus, calling him from (the profession of) catching physical fish, had said, "Follow me, and I will make you fishers (*sic*) of men." So, because he made Peter and other apostles into fishers of men, he gave them also nets for this different kind of fishing. And these nets are first of all Christ's, then Peter's, and they are the work of Christ or his law, as well as the Holy Scripture given out by God, from which men willing to learn can be instructed.

Thus the Holy Scriptures are woven and prepared like a physical net, one knot tied to another, until the whole great net is made; similarly, there are tied one to another the different truths of the Holy Scripture, so that they can enclose a multitude of believers (and every single believer with all his spiritual and physical gifts in order that, surrounded by the net, he might be drawn out of the ocean of this world). And this net is capable of pulling out everyone from the sea of deep and gross sins.

Now we can understand that this net began to break not so much for the multitude of things caught – like Peter's net – but, just as in a physical sea, a great number of other repellent things get caught in the net, so also a number of lost souls, heretics and offenders, enter the net of faith (sometimes outwardly being of the faith but later – in times of temptation – reverting to abominations and heresies). Such (people) tear the net, and the more evil-doers enter the net; the more the latter is torn and ripped. The faith in God and the words of God perish between them; for they profess God and our Lord Jesus Christ with their lips only, holiness remaining an outward thing with them. And the devil goes slyly about with these erring people, seeking how to help them to enter the net falsely. And then they tear it (the devil always doing it in such a way as to have at least some parts of the net on his side – for instance holy baptism and other sacraments – so that he would not appear quite as naked as a pagan. But otherwise he tears all the truths of the Holy Scripture).

Yet this net is capable of encompassing a great multitude of believers and of the elect, even though they were countless thousands, their multitude does not tear the net that is made of many truths of the Holy Scripture. For faith does not weaken nor suffer from great numbers of believers. It thrives and becomes stronger because of them, since every one of the believers strengthens and broadens faith (because he lives by faith which in turn becomes a help and an example to others). If one of them should perchance weaken in his faith, the others will immediately seek to help. Therefore a multitude of believers is the power and the strength of faith.

This net can draw out of the sea of (our) world and its depths of sins only those who to the end remain in the net, not tearing a single part of it. For wherever they would damage the net by breaking one of the truths out of which it is knotted together, they would be unable to remain within, and would drown in the depth of the sea. Only he can be drawn out who is willing to let himself be pulled out where the fishermen intend it; if he resists the net (or the direction), he cannot be pulled out.

CHAPTER 3

INTERPRETATION OF THE MIRACULOUS FISHING (CONCLUSION)

But here is a doubt as to who are the true fishermen of Christ. For there are many of whom it is thought that they are Christ's, but they put down their nets for a haul in the sea at night, and they do it for a year, for two years, for ten and even more years, without catching anything, because they fish at night and because their nets are torn; indeed, the nets are a patchwork of rotten strings, mixed up with reasonings of different people, unsteady. (And there are those who weave their nets out of such materials).

And many might say, "We have been fishing night after night, and yet we cannot be sure that we have caught a single soul to repentance." Many of them catch a whole community for their own advantage, feeding their bellies on the produce of other people's estates, shearing wool and getting the cream of the milk, and abandoning the weakest cattle to rapacious animals. Woe to them and their fishing.

Peter's net, however, is his faith in Christ, established on his words, by which man can be drawn out of the deep sea of this world and its wickedness. Just as in a real physical sea, there are fish dwelling in dark hollow depths, so in this world of ours there are people living as if in a thick darkness, unable to see either overhead nor in front of them, distinguishing nothing on their left and nothing on their right, unable to put their feet forward with one step of certainty, but always afraid lest a fall, an accident, or an error overtake them. Peter's net is therefore the only thing left to man in order to save his life from such a danger; to it he can cling in the darkness of the marine depths and eschew the evil which surrounds man everywhere…

For a gorged and surfeited man is driven to and fro by the mighty currents like a boat, relentlessly tossed with no respite; his desires move him constantly on, and bring to him more and new desires, yearnings after change, licentiousness, roguery, and loose living; he is irritated by trifles, powerless in his anger, constantly harassed and afraid of something; sometimes hysterically rejoicing, yet at the same time burdened and insecure within himself. And so, moved by this or the other evil, he stands in the midst of the world and its devils who are ready to devour him. (They find a way to him either through evil passions, material gain, anger, hate, shame, false modesty, pride, daring, fear, doubt, or some other transgression from the path of God). And all this is apart from the other snares running through the world as temptations and visible injustices. That is why Peter's net of faith is so necessary; with it he has pulled many out of the depth of the sea, out of the dangerous onslaughts of devilish waves.

Who is in the net and who lets himself be pulled out of the depths of the sea? No one else can be thought of but he who thinks and desires but to live by faith in every phase of his life, (and who desires) to know when and where the devil is pulling; (it can be only he) who rests to consult the Scripture just as blind men stop in darkness, not daring to go on unless someone take them by their hand to lead them into safety. Such is the character of faith that we can call nothing right or wrong unless we look at it through faith; and faith will tell us whether it is right or wrong. In the same way, we cannot judge things spiritual and divine except by faith, as was said by Saint Paul,Faith is (the assurance) of things unseen, in which we have hope.

We believe that God is the Holy Trinity: Father, Son, and the Holy Spirit; one God, Creator of heaven and earth, and that Christ the Son of God is truly God and truly man, begotten by the Holy Spirit in the Virgin Mary and born of her; we believe also in other things spiritual and heavenly and future, in the resurrection of the (dead, both the) good and the wicked. We can touch upon these things which are distant and invisible only through a faith based on the words of God, because we are placed in complete darkness as it were, far away from those things which we can neither ascertain nor see except by faith, and that dimly.

Thus faith is necessary for all things, for without faith no man can please God. Wherever man moves without faith it is as if he jumped into a dark abyss; in that very moment his own error catches him.

CHAPTER 4

THE INTERPRETATION OF THE LAW

This useful knowledge about faith presupposes a foundation on the words of God. When a man believes in God he believes also in His words. And believing that He is the unchangeable God, he also believes that His words cannot change that which they affirm, that is: whoever fulfills them has the grace of God (upon him) and is blessed in everything he possesses; and whoever transgresses the words of God (commits) mortal sin and incurs the wrath of God and is cursed in everything he possesses. This aspect of faith could bring about much good for people as well as an obligation to avoid falling under the wrath of God because of the guilt of mortal sin; by keeping His word they do His will and stand in His grace and His blessing is only upon those who believe and act (in accordance with their faith). These things are (valid) for those whose faith is full of wisdom and life, in whom dwell the fear and the love of God; a dead or blind faith cannot have these things.

Saint Paul says about faith that it comes from what is heard, and what is heard comes by the preaching of (the words of) Jesus Christ.

The sense of this is that, even though faith is founded on every word of God, it is valid for us Christians only if it agrees with the original intention of Christ. For the Jewish law has an insufficiency (when judged by) the law of Christ since it observes material sacrifices and other physical requirements that the old law showed them in material parables. And as these parables foreshadowed Christ, they became true in Christ.

Judging from this point of view, we can understand that many divine words of the first law do not bind us (for instance) to follow the lambs; but because lambs symbolized Christ the true sacrifice for sins, we must accept them as such, since Christ brought to us this more suitable faith. It is therefore right that faith comes from hearing the word of Jesus Christ and that the Scripture should be understood and obeyed in accordance with the words of Christ and his truth. His words are for our edification and they will confirm the infallibility of his teaching.

Jewish as well as other human scriptures can be based pretentiously and falsely on Christ's words and his examples; these false scriptures are added to Christ and his words in order to lie more successfully and acceptably 'through Christ.' It is indeed imperative to judge any teaching by the words of Christ and by his life, to see whether it agrees with his examples and words. A wise man, considering all these things and establishing their agreement with the teaching of Christ, will have true faith.

CHAPTER 5

FAITH AND SUPERSTITION

There are many things attributed to faith or said to be of faith that are not faith, nor do they resemble it. For the worst time has come, a time in which people know so little about faith that they hold Christian faith to be a heresy, while heresies they often parade around as faith. And this is the great division of the people today; there are two parties that anathematize one another. The straying away from faith has long since become a great movement, and the people are so much steeped in errors that they accept dead, erroneous, and man-made customs introduced as faith. And they are so ignorant that true faith appears to them as a foul heresy. Battles and disputes, murders, arson, and many other evils – these are the sins that the people have brought upon themselves. And evil men became all the more hardened with a deep hatred against the true faith. For this reason they now recognize faith with difficulty, as it has been all befouled by heresies, animosities, and ignominies committed in her name.

It is necessary to maintain the sense of ancient wise men in such chaotic conditions in which heresy is honored as faith in order to be ready to believe that which God desires, and to disbelieve what God does not want…

Whoever harbors any doubt in this matter and says, "I do not know what He believed or disbelieved," should use right reasoning; for, if it could not be known, nobody could ever have believed. There have been many, however, who have believed the way He desired it; many have been the followers of the faith once given to the saints by its author and perfecter, Jesus Christ. His will is that one should believe His law which he left through His apostles and those parts of the older Scriptures which can reveal other truths in Christ. This, then, is faith divine and Christian, for faith is necessary for all things that have been commanded for observance. Nobody could be faithful to them unless he first believed in God and His words – they guide and teach man. Observing these things as Christ has commanded him in his law, man shall live by faith. And all information about faith is preserved in the law of God; therein we find

70

what we must believe and what we must not believe. And just as faith given by God can be insulted by one who is contemptuous of it or unwilling to submit to it with acts of obeisance, so it can also be outraged by him who pays obeisance to strange things contrary to the faith of God. And, since He has given to His saints only one faith which is sufficient, it is clear that any other faith of which He is not the author is contrary to His will. He does not want any believing contrary to His own faith. For Lord Jesus said, "Have faith in God."

(In consequence of the fact) that so many heterodox and foreign beliefs have long ago been disseminated and a multitude of peoples forced by threat of anathema to follow them, it is all the more necessary for conscientious people to study and examine their faith in God and His law, to rededicate their hearts to it, and to analyze the other faiths in order to see where these are leading their followers. For the Pope requires that his person, his letters, and his laws be given credence as the law of God. He writes, for instance, letters to countries and regions, sending them on (paper) sheets his forgiveness of all sins and remission of all suffering in exchange for money. And anyone who would disbelieve these letters and doubt their authority he would burn. And what is more, the Pope regards his letters and laws far superior to those of God; for he punishes the transgressions of his laws, not the transgressions of God's laws. On the contrary, he burns those who obey God's laws.

And there are not only heterodox beliefs but, in addition to them, all sorts of books which are clearly against the divine law, yet they are honored as if they were of the true faith. What a lot of fraudulent miracles there are in passion books of the saints and other annals, venerated by misguided people! And what uncertain conjectures and untruthful, vague reasonings are held by men as faith! And they have mixed up even true faith with these conjectures and reasonings to such an extent that this medley is put on a pedestal as real faith, while the living faith is thrown into darkness and violated. It is of necessity therefore that the apostle says:

I appeal to you to contend for the faith that was once and for all delivered to the saints. For admission has been secretly gained by some whom long ago were designated for this condemnation, ungodly persons who pervert the grace of our God into licentiousness.

He admonishes and appeals to them to contend for the one and true faith which was given to the saints, the reason for it being – as he says – that admission has been secretly gained by ungodly persons who perverted the grace of our God into licentiousness, conjectural thinking, and who denied our Lord Jesus Christ. Such persons have harmfully distorted our faith. And if someone today would try to find out what it was that these deniers have discovered by their multiple distortions and confusion of faith (so that they are even unable to detect its beginning or end), he would certainly have ample reason to say, "Contend for the one holy faith which was given to the saints!"

But against whom should they contend for a faith that they not only deny but also even dominate – just as they try to dominate people? He who does not incur suffering from the deniers on account of faith will be a rare person indeed, for they are powerful enemies of faith underneath the skin of faith. If you are a man of no account, do not pick up a quarrel with them lest you meet their challenge. However, do not interpret this contending for faith as a sort of gambling wager; but whosoever is able to overcome the unwise enemies by truth, without querulous censoriousness, let him do so. In such a contending for faith we can gain advantage, because we must resist all such who tear the net of faith, everyone who tries to drag the net in his own direction forcing everyone else to go his way, and all those who try to rule over others inflicting upon them their faith which they have twisted and fixed up to fit their own needs. Do not give in to the fabricators of faith and to those who sow confusion. Who, knowing true faith, would want to follow perfidy?

CHAPTER 6

THE PERFECT APOSTOLIC CHURCH

This (kind) of declaration is followed immediately by disfavor, because the powerful enemies of faith, reigning over faith, dictate its limits and do what they want with it. If a poor fellow does not believe what the mighty in the seats of power measure out for him to believe, he will certainly fall into their hands as a heretic who dares impertinently to follow the whims of his own conscience, rebelliously refusing to accept the conclusions of the heads in authority. Death sits in the shadow of such authority. And if she should, jumping out of the shadow, strangle one of us, others will be scared. Therefore it seems to some that they are truer to faith than many priests if they maintain external order and peace with the exercise of authority over faith. But when they are betrayed, God will be with them only who persevere in times of trouble. For I say without hesitation that he who is afraid to die for faith at the hands of domestic enemies, will not persevere in faith, unless God should in some way shorten this evil time.

What has been said in the preceding chapter about faith is based on the fact that Peter is the spiritual fisherman and that his net is the law of Christ or the religion of Christ tied to his law by many knots of different truths of divine words; that the whole net is sufficient to fish the sinful and to draw them out of the marine depths of the sins of this world and finally to prepare the 'fishes,' (that is) the saintly people, for God's purposes.

In the example of saint Peter and of other apostles we see that they are fishermen of a (spiritual) fishing established by Jesus and that he has given them such a net of faith in his words when he said, I have given them the words that you gave me, and they have received them … and the world has hated them.

Therefore he sent them the Holy Spirit who made them speak the words of God; through them the apostles have established faith to be preached in the whole world for full salvation. Thus the fishermen of spiritual fishing, having the nets made by the Holy Spirit, were sent by our Lord Jesus to go into the whole world and preach the gospel to the whole human creation in order that those who believe might be baptized and saved; and those who refuse to believe or to be filled by his reality will be condemned. For faith apart from works is dead, useless, and devilish; real faith is alive, useful, and Christian. Jesus has sent his disciples into the whole world with this faith and this message that they might teach good and useful works to

73

every man through the reading of Christ's truth. It is as Saint Paul confesses about himself and other apostles:

Christ Jesus (who is) in you, him we proclaim to you, warning every man and teaching every man in all wisdom, that we may present every man perfect in Christ Jesus.

Therefore the apostles taught unrelentingly all people to believe through the truth of the gospel. And because they taught in this way (that every man should be perfect in Christ Jesus), therefore, as Jesus said to them, I chose you and appointed you that you should go and bear fruit and that your fruit should abide.

Let us see (whether and) where their fishing with the net of faith has been successful, bearing fruit of eternal life. Through their teaching they have established a perfect community of faith and life; this people has remained an example to all future faithful Christians, so that all believers can look back to these first Christians and discover in them the evident fruit of apostolic labor, as well as a useful and abiding certainty for their own times. Reason will show that here the apostles' work bore fruit in accordance with the purposes of Christ... The future generations can safely emulate their work and expect eternal life.

It is therefore necessary to see where these people were confirmed in their faith and how they were established. In the *Acts of the Apostles* and other recorded writings we can find that there were believing people in the apostolic days and that their preaching went into the whole world so that there was no nation in which their voice was not heard. From this we can surmise that in every nation and language there was someone who believed the gospel through the apostolic preaching. I am not saying that all were believers who heard the apostles preach, but everywhere there were some whom God had chosen; here more, there less. According to the *Acts of the Apostles* these groups in cities, villages, and all regions of the world were called congregations of believers that united all those of the same faith. The apostles have set these congregations apart from other unbelieving peoples. They did not necessarily live apart physically, in a special district of the same city, but they were united in one fellowship of faith, which they manifested in common participation in matters spiritual and religious. Because of this common fellowship and sharing of faith and of the word of God they have been called congregations, communities of believers. And in the days when the apostles were preaching, the Romans and their lords ruled over wide the parts of the world: in the Jewish lands, in Greece, in Syria, and other countries, as can be found in the *Acts of the Apostles*. And in this entire realm the Jews were interspersed among the Gentiles. Thus, when the apostles preached the gospel, they spoke to a two-fold people. So, when some were converted, some came from the Jews and some from the Gentiles; both, separating themselves from (the pagans and Jews) their former co-religionists, they became a third people of a different faith. Therefore the Christians, a people set apart, were often servants among Gentiles as well as Jews, all of them paying taxes to the Romans.

These people, believing in Christ, were organized in two manners or fashions by the apostles. One was the outward, material aspect of making them live properly together among this two-fold and hostile people in a manner befitting saints. They were told therefore to pay their taxes to the highest authorities and to obey them in all reasonable matters so as not to give opportunity for the pagan rulers and tax lords to say, "They are proud (these Christians), they themselves want to be lords, ruling over our possessions." In such a case they would immediately attack them and their gospel faith and forbid the preaching of Christ's gospel on their domains. The apostles saw to it therefore that the Christians were to be subject to the authorities in all material matters of service, paying their taxes and toll-money and due respect.

Secondly, they were to live humbly among Gentiles and Jews, conducting themselves in an exemplary way, as Saint Peter had taught them:

Maintain good conduct among the Gentiles, so that in case they speak against you as wrongdoers, they may see your good deeds and glorify God on the day of visitation.

By such correct, meek, and exemplary living they would get along much better with their fellow Gentiles and Jews, avoiding all cause for complaint, dissatisfaction, irritation, anger, and underhanded behavior. For kindly and non-hurtful living can charm and tame even pagans disposed to aggression. It was precisely this humble and loving behavior which effected the conversion of the Gentiles and Jews to faith, because good examples move the unbelievers sometimes more forcibly than preaching and long speeches, and deeds are more effective than words. For this reason the apostles established such a behavior among the believers that they might be without reproach among a people susceptible to anger. They should be an example to them with their kindliness; however, if this goodness were not to succeed and if God allowed the Gentiles and Jews to attack them, the Christians should not defend themselves but humbly bear all injustices inflicted upon them.

These are external rules, yet they are sufficiently established by divine orders. The apostles had a perfect net of faith and into this perfection they drew people out of the depths of the sea of sins and errors. And whoever was drawn out of the sea could not live in any other way than by faith alone, rendering to God faith and love, and preserving for himself an innocent conscience. Abundant evidences of this are found in the apostolic teaching, in their net as it were. But the most important thing expected of the pagans converted to Christ was that they be renewed, casting off their old life of Adam which is corrupt and deceitful, and putting on the new nature of Jesus Christ. Idolatry and drunkenness, debauchery and licentiousness, quarreling and jealousy, murdering, and other evils – these are the deeds of the old man, of the first, damned man in whom all died and of whom all are born under God's anger; that is why they must cast off first this old man and then put on the new man Jesus Christ, which means putting on the honesty of his life, according to the gifts of God's grace.

This ability to imitate Christ in his honest life, his innocence in humility, his reverence to God, and his justice, is given in different degrees to different people; some are more endowed than others; but they all must arrive at a newness of life so as not to give a single chance to the old life to introduce mortal sin. For wherever virtue is damaged, mortal sin remains in its stead; and man is obliged to defend it (the virtue). This is why man must constantly put off his old nature, lest his transgressions remain with him. And to put on new life means to follow Christ either in a more perfect or more simple way, obeying in every respect the commandments of God to which he is bound under the penalty of mortal sin.

These things were presented for the first time to this people, (but) on the foundation of Christ's gospel. For even a Jew could do similar things but, not being based on the foundation of Christ, these things would have no meaning. The cornerstone, therefore, must be Christ, through whom faith, grace, and life shall prosper. Saint Paul gave this foundation to the first Christians when he said, For no other foundation can any one lay than that which is laid, which is Christ. Let each man take care how he builds upon it.

The soundest and surest foundation has been laid out to this people in order that every good work is firmly and unshakably established. On this foundation stand the true apostles of Christ and the prophets as well as those first Christians. It is for this reason that we of the latter day hold these original Christians before us for example and assurances let us stand ourselves on the same firm and mighty foundation which was built for them by the apostles. For today there are many other foundations, built in later times, and they are all insecure and bad. The Pope (for instance) wants to be the foundation of the Holy Church and her head and her cornerstone; every one of the monkish orders finds the foundation of its rule in its first monk; and there are hosts of such foundations. And the straying people do not seek (truth) but only follows dead customs, walking in the (footsteps) of their fathers who have invented the customs; the people are born unto customs just as pagans are born unto idols. In such circumstances it is therefore best for wise men to look for the foundation that the apostles had made for the original Christians, in order that they might continue their good works.

CHAPTER 7

THE PERFECT APOSTOLIC CHURCH (CONTINUED)

We can learn, furthermore, that the apostles have instituted this people in equality, without undue compulsory respect among themselves, with the only (demand) that they love and serve each other like one body composed of many members, Christ being the head. For we are taught that, being many, we are the members of one body, communing and sharing the one bread which is the body of Christ; let us, therefore, live as members of one body, serving each other voluntarily, being mutually useful without forced compulsion, and admonishing one another. In those days of Gentile government ruling over people with coercive power, no one among the first Christians would willingly be administrators, or mayors, or councilors, or judges in courts of disputes.

Even though under pagan might, they were set apart because of their faith; they were subject to them only with regard to paying taxes. They refused to adapt their religion and morals to pagan authority. Because of this, none of them ever held an official position, none of them ever practiced the profession of executioners, bailiffs, councilors, mayors or ruling lords; yet, at the same time, they all, brethren of the same faith and partakers of Christ, submitted in all material and civil matters to pagans exercising such professions.

The congregations of Christ lived among pagans and existed without holding temporal power for over three hundred years until the time of Constantine. He was the first one who infiltrated himself into the Christian community with Gentile rule and Gentile (system of) clerks. The apostles, however, taught their people to look after higher and more perfect things than the pagans were seeking. From the teaching of the apostles we learn that they asked them to lead a life worthy of the calling with all lowliness and meekness, with patience, forbearing one another in love, eager to maintain the unity of the Spirit in the bond of peace. There is one Lord, one faith, one baptism, one God and Father of us all.

This kind of administration is far different from the pagan administration that has to resort to civil laws and pagan clerks and officials. It is a much loftier and nobler law to be like one body and to be governed by the same spirit of God in all matters divine and spiritual and moral, having only one Lord, Jesus Christ; a pagan government is bound to weaken justice since it attracts men who are not wise or desirous of the common good. Pagan and temporal rule is far surpassed by those who through grace and good will are realizing God's pleasing truth so that it might dwell on earth as it is in eternity.

CHAPTER 8

THE PERFECT APOSTOLIC CHURCH (CONTINUED)

Christians cannot be followers of Christ's faith if they are obeying another authority, pagan and civil, standing in courthouses with lawsuits; they cannot have the fellowship of Christ and be saved if they die in this (acceptance of authority). The enemy which is the pagan and worldly spirit may contradict this by saying, "Well, if these Christian congregations are not governed by temporal authority in matters of faith and morals, but only by mutual love, what then if they lack love and if some injustice were done to them? And did not many of them resort to courts? Did not Saint Paul say to them, 'If you have such cases, why do you lay them before those who are least esteemed by the church?' And so they availed themselves of pagan offices and supplied their officials, love not being adequate."

To this can be proffered the following answer: it is true that the apostles brought the first Christians to these perfect things, instituting that everything be done through divine love. The correctness and truth of this commandment has not been lessened simply because there were some among them who were as imperfect as small children not yet ready to digest substantial food and clamoring only for milk. Indeed, many a person, converted to the faith of Christ from the Gentiles or Jews, accustomed as he had been to evil and inclined rather strongly toward

79

temporal arrangements, even though believing in the Son of God and His truth, did not become immediately perfect in his faith. Among such converts there were some who had many imperfections and whom the apostles rebuked, but they were tolerated in part for the hope that they would improve in time. Saint Paul saw the disorders of some weak believers; yes, he even saw a Christian bringing action against another Christian and both sitting under judgment before pagan court officials. And he said to them,Do you not know that the saints will judge this world? And if the world is to be judged by you, are you incompetent to try trivial cases?

And, rebuking them with these words, he still patiently tolerated their weakness in the hope that they would reform, and allowed them to settle their differences at home rather than to go to law before pagans. He could not bring them to perfection because of their weakness, and so he very patiently conceded to them the choice of the lesser evil, as long as they had to put up with evil at all. It is a greater evil for Christians to bring their grievances concerning temporal matters before pagans, but it is a lesser evil for them to reveal their shame at home before their own people. It is always an evil, though. And (the apostle) said to them that any grievance is evil, even when he conceded to them the possibility of a court (administered through the inner) domestic circle. Says he,I say this to your shame. Therefore I give this to you as an eternal law: do not go to courts. But I concede you your shame that you may bear it as long as your mind is uncircumcised, gravitating unduly toward earthly matters, and filled with grievances.

When that mind shall blush from shame and run away from evil, then will the wise one be able, through the gift of divine grace, to scorn that which drove him to courts. It is clear that the eternal law does not admit lawsuits. Even Saint Paul could not boast of their faith and obedience, when the congregations were standing before him in shame, with grievances and lawsuits concerning earthly goods. He speaks to them wisely, therefore, trying to help them when he says,Can it be that there is no man among you wise enough to decide between members of the brotherhood, but brother goes to law against brother, and that before unbelievers? To have lawsuits at all with one another is defeat for you.

80

Why not rather suffer wrong? Instead, you yourselves wrong and defraud, and that even among your own brethren. Is there no man among you wise enough to decide between brother and brother?

He is not thinking here of a Gentile court of justice according to whose pattern one of the wiser members would become judge and settle the case between brother and brother, for such a court is based on coercive power, and all those who want their case decided before a court must submit themselves to the jury. (He is thinking) of something much simpler and closer to truth when he says, "Can it be that there is no man wise enough among you to decide between members of the brotherhood? Have you become so poor in wisdom?" He knows that they have more sense (than that) because he gives thanks to God that in every way they were enriched in Him with all speech and all knowledge. And to those enriched with knowledge of chastisement he says, "Why, having wisdom and knowledge, do you not decide between members of the brotherhood in accordance with the gospel, endeavoring to do away with the grievances?" Here judgment means the recognition of injustice and the elimination of injustice first by administering an admonition and, second, by bringing the brothers to peace by reconciliation and forgiveness of injustice.

If there has been committed an injustice that could be remedied by material restoration, the guilty brother should use this form of reconciliation with the innocent one. If there have been insults deceitfully and publicly defaming the good reputation of a brother, the defendant should be moved to blot out the false accusation in the presence of others. If, however, the defamation has spread through the region, even that base infamy should be forgiven. In all cases of wrongdoing which take place among the brethren, the guilty party should be admonished with a reprimand, and the guilty should humbly ask forgiveness, for there is no other way of absolving an injustice. Both brethren should forget the committed wrongs so that, through reconciliation, love and peace might prevail. It is much wiser to settle differences between brothers in this way. However, this (method) can succeed only among men of good will who are filled with humility and fear of God and a disposition to submit to truth revealed to them by wise men.

The apostle has in mind the kind of goodness that all those who call themselves brethren in Christ should share, being set apart from the world. But cruel, covetous, vindictive horned goats, clothed in robes of worldly wisdom know how to extricate themselves from guilt in court-houses, they know how to cover up their iniquities and how to put blame on others, while the innocent ones are then summoned to magistrates and courts where they are examined, fined, tied to whipping-posts, and pilloried. No, those evil-doers deserve to be burned standing before those gods (*sic*) to whom they ran with their indictments. The best court for brethren would be to dispense justice on the basis of goodness, which alone would advance and improve brotherly consciences in true virtue.

CHAPTER 9

THE PERFECT APOSTOLIC CHURCH (CONTINUED)

Magistrates and courts deal with sins, even though officially with property matters; they add the evil of sins because of the corruption of consciences. For this reason Saint Paul reprimands the early Christians like children in Christ because of their lawsuits (concerning worldly goods only) in courts before infidel pagans. He says,To have lawsuits at all with one another is sin for you. Why not rather suffer wrong?

He clearly considers as sin lawsuits concerning corporeal goods. Of what use is their faith, then, if they are in sin because of lawsuits? Did they not believe in the Son of God in order to be saved from their sins and from the devil's power through his death? Why, now because of material gain they jeopardize and lose all that which they had gained through Christ's death; his death is wasted on them unless they earn their right to it by a new repentance. And they cannot repent from their sins unless they give up their lawsuits. This is to show that man can be Christian only if he commits no wrong and harms no one, and if he meekly suffers the wrongdoing of others, not returning evil for evil in accordance with the commandment of Christ. Neither must he have on his conscience the death of a single person.

We have tarried longer upon these matters in order to show that the apostles, while preaching perfection to the first Christians, could not bring them instantly to that perfection – that is, not all of them – and so they offered them a concession in time, hoping that they would thus bring them eventually to the better goal. So now Saint Paul concedes courts at least at home, away from pagans – and even these courts he conceded with shame. But in his last letters to these people we find that all this has been corrected.

And more time was spent on this also in order to show that the early Christians established their rules concerning lawsuits and courts on the words of Saint Paul saying,If, then, you have such cases, why do you lay them before those who are least esteemed by the Church? I say this to your shame!

In establishing these rules about lawsuits and courts they completely distorted the words of Saint Paul, giving them the opposite meaning. Thus, not the least esteemed, but the most esteemed of these confused people are chosen for judges in courts. And a priest who should be an expert of the gospel and castigate therefore this error on the basis of the gospel, goes himself to the court, elevates their shame into honor, and chooses councilors for this shame, thinking it advantageous for faith if this shame is conducted (administered) wisely.

CHAPTER 10

THE PERFECT APOSTOLIC CHURCH (CONTINUED)

We began our study by showing how the apostles established the first Christians in faith through the perfection of the law of God, which is set apart from the pagan laws administered by temporal powers. This is evident from the things taught by Christ's law when evil arises among faithful Christians, such as the appearance of adversaries, defilers, and heretics among their own ranks. Christ's commandment says that such should be instructed, admonished, and reprimanded for the purpose of rehabilitation. And Jesus Christ wisely teaches that this be done confidentially, between him that admonishes and the guilty brother. If he listens and accepts the admonition, says Lord Jesus, (the admonisher) has gained a brother.

But if he does not listen, take one or two others along with you, that every word may be confirmed by the evidence of two or three witnesses. If he listens to these, you have gained him.

If he refuses to listen to them, tell it to the whole church of the faithful, for the multitude may cause him to feel shame and, convinced by the truth of their arguments, he may be won over. And if he refuses to listen even to this multitude and scorns its admonition, let him be to you as a Gentile and a flagrant sinner, avoid him, and have no Christian fellowship with him. With the same reasoning Saint Paul says:

I wrote to you in my letter not to associate with immoral men; not at all meaning the immoral of this world, or the greedy, or robbers, or idolaters, but rather I wrote to you not to associate with any one who bears the name of brother if he is guilty of immorality or greed, or is an idolater, reviler, drunkard, or robber – not even to eat with such a one.

He forbids associating, eating, and drinking with them; that is, he commands us to segregate ourselves from them… And he speaks also of loafers and busybodies who are not busy; do not associate with them, but let them keep quiet and earn their own bread they have to eat. Let no one look after somebody else's bread.

All these things are based on Christ's purity and perfection, which the apostles have promulgated among the early Christians who lived simply on the foundation of Christ's words. It must be apparent to all wise men that Christ's perfection is preached to a fallen human generation – fallen because of the pagan rule of the kings of earthly realms and (their) civil administrators. Yet, as was said before, malefactors cannot be compelled to punishment for their sins, nor is vengeance allowed upon them; through brotherly love alone can they be brought to repentance and redeemed. This is the plain good news which proclaims that a sinner can again obtain divine grace after he had lost it through his sinning; yes, he can even be saved while, on the contrary, civil administration everywhere administers death to men for such offences without giving them (a chance) to reform.

The confused people of this world act so badly that, while they bemoan iniquities and material damages, they are ready to murder human beings on their account. This killing of humans is the way of the people of the world, who love the world, who pity the world for all the wrongs that befall it. Yet they can have no communion with Christ. In the first Christian community, however, if brotherly love mended not the way of the guilty, the people did not associate with him, eschewing him. If they were unable to help him and to move him to repentance, still they caused him no evil by adding murder to his sins. They separated themselves from him, remaining without guilt. But the heathenish civil administration does just the opposite: it does nothing good for evil; all it cares about is to murder the evil one, and to throw the burden of his sins on those who render evil for evil.

CHAPTER 11

THE PERFECT APOSTOLIC CHURCH (CONTINUED)

When we look at the first Christians, we see that they were sufficiently grounded in faith in accordance with the law of Christ. For this law is of itself quite sufficient and adequate for a redeeming administration of God's people; indeed, only through the exercise of this law can there be brought to the people of God that true innocence which God loves in them; holding to this law they will unflinchingly seek Him with all their heart and cultivate justice and love for all peoples, be they friends or enemies, wishing no one ill or injury, and if same were done to them by others, they will suffer it without revenge, not returning evil for evil to either friend or foe, for in all this consists the doctrine of Christ. And if there are some who do not desire to hold fast to these things, they are not righteous in the sight of God.

It is improbable therefore that the worldly people who love the world and desire to live for the things of this world would pay allegiance to this law. Those who want to abide by the law (of Christ) must give up the world completely. The first congregations of God prospered in the law of Christ because they completely abandoned pagan errors as well as Jewish unbelief and all vanities of this world; and lo, they grew in spiritual prosperity and increased in numbers of just followers in spite of all lawless adversities of the civil administration, even carrying on without the law of the highest priest, but simply governing themselves by the law of Christ.

But later, when the two other laws were added, namely the temporal and the papal law, the Christian society immediately deteriorated in its quality and perished. They who write chronicles are stressing this, and we see it with our own bare eyes that these two laws are the most injurious corruption intent upon killing the faith and the law of God. Therefore we of this generation, sitting as it were under the shadow of these laws, discuss weakly the law of God or His rule, because the darkness of these laws has befogged our eyes. And so, groping our way in the dark, we guess and wonder: if the doctrine of Christ is sufficient by itself, without the addition of human laws, can it restore here on earth the full Christian religion? We ask this in fear, and with trembling we affirm it because this law of Christ was adequate to institute a Christian humanity with all his disciples and without the admixture of human institutions.

By the same token, this law is not less effective today than it was in that era, nor is it weakened by the resistance of many, but rather all the more strengthened. And so it is always sufficient. Furthermore, the sufficiency of Christ's law was not exhausted by the behavior of rebellious people in the original Holy Church; on the contrary, it was always adequate to convert multitudes to the apostolic life – and no one can be converted except through this law. Therefore, if the law was sufficient to convert unbelievers to faith, it is all the more adequate to reform life and morals as this is much easier. For this reason the law of Christ was sufficient in itself to establish as well as to maintain the whole church of God in every material and spiritual aspect. And the rule of Christ's religion is better than the rule of human admixtures. Who then, will deny that the bride of Christ is more perfect and according to the law of God, than were she nurtured by the admixtures of human laws, which are as poison? Life in God is secure, but if human laws are mixed with it, divine laws become unintelligible, and men finally abandon them. Christ has commanded his bride to keep this law under the penalty of mortal sin; that means, she cannot abandon him or otherwise abolish (his laws) without committing mortal sin.

CHAPTER 12

THE PERFECT APOSTOLIC CHURCH (CONCLUSION)

This is the reason why we expound as much as we can, yet still too weakly, the sufficiency of the law of Christ; we pour it on the sores of the wounded ones who are outside the law, having fallen among robbers who stripped them and beat them. Yes, this law shines brightly like a light in the darkness and the apostles announced its sufficiency to this rebellious people of yore. And. they succeeded so well that they could say with justification, "Stand firm thus in the Lord, our beloved!" Otherwise, had they not been successful in establishing Christian faith and virtues, they could not have said this. They could not have spoken of standing firm if these people had not been firm at that time. Moreover, this "standing firm" implies an obligation to hold fast to what they had been taught. That is the great certainty which they proclaimed saying,But if even we, or an angel from heaven, should preach to you a gospel contrary to that which we preached to you, let him be accursed. As we have said before, so now I say again, if anyone is preaching to you a gospel contrary to that which you received, let him be accursed!

He would curse not only them but also even himself and, yes, even the angel from heaven if he were to teach otherwise. This places the teaching on a firm foundation and that foundation was given to the early Christians in accordance with the law of Christ. And even a heavenly angel could not have taught it better than the Son of God and the apostles after him. Where the word of the Gospel is accepted, there faith is made sure and the law of God is strengthened.

Those Christian churches stood in the midst of a pagan people, they followed the Gospel teaching, surrounded by great temptations, yet they remained faithful to the apostolic teaching according to Christ for over three hundred years after Christ's ascension. And they prospered in spiritual treasures while they held fast to that teaching. For they excelled in numerous and victorious martyrdoms; all the highest bishops beginning with Peter and ending with Sylvester suffered for (the sake of) faith, and there were thirty-five of them holding Saint Peter's position. Every one of them, one after another, suffered martyrdom at the hands of Roman princes, and with them a great host of priests and clergymen as well as laymen of both sexes. These all suffered tortures and cruelties with utmost courage until the most terrible death, joyously, for Christ's sake. Nothing but the true foundation of faith is manifested in these perfect Christian acts. It was this absolute certainty in faith which made them voluntarily undergo martyrdom and any other evil from the world; all we have today is the certainty of a great falling away from faith because of the impatience of priests and lay people.

(Today) all and sundry live in duplicity, inventing stratagems in relation to faith, endeavoring to be included in it in whatever way as long as they can have their fling and fatten their bellies. They are after favors and peace with the world, cajoling it with pleasantries since they do not want to suffer from it in any respect. And so it is that if we compare our present life of faith to that of the early Church it is like putting darkness against light. For this reason have we recalled to our mind those in whom faith was established infallibly through the apostles; let us see now if there are still some Christians willing to return to the ways of the first Church, and to follow its faith without mental reservations, in patience and with sincerity of heart.

CHAPTER 13

REFUTATION OF THE CLAIMS OF THE COUNCIL OF BASEL

AND OF THE ARGUMENTS OF JUAN PALOMAR

Now all these words with which I praised the early Church of Christ stink (to the nostrils) of the Church of Rome as ugly heresies. This is the why and the wherefore of the vituperations of the Master Auditor at Basel when the Czechs had proved the use of the chalice of God by the original Holy Church, showing that this Church truly maintained the practice of the divine chalice. And yet this Master Auditor of the Papal Court found fault with this argument, calling it brittle, weak, and harmful, and in many other ways bringing up sly objections and difficult obloquies.

He even said – among many other things – that the early Christian Church was stupid and in a sad condition, while admitting that in holy matters and in its zeal of faith it was wonderful. For "the polished and dignified church of ritual, beauty, and splendor came after the plain apostolic church of divine honesty in the same way as rams' skins dyed red came after badgers' skins for tent covering." Not only divine honesty and sacramental customs but even faith of old times were explained in such a manner as to make them appear doubtful or unknown when applied to the original apostolic Church. And yet it is to this Holy Church that Jesus Christ promised his constant presence: "Lo, I am with you to the end of the world." Concerning this Saint Augustine says – and he is quoted by Saint Thomas: "I am with you to the end of the world; this has been said to the entire Holy Church in which some die and others are born, until now and to the close of the age." This, too, was quoted by the Auditor.

Wise men ought to pay attention, therefore, to the pronouncements of this master because, when he divides so cunningly the present condition of the Church from that of the early Church, attributing everything good to the former and all weaknesses to the latter, he speaks to the detriment and debasement of the early Holy Church. He labels it with stupidity and ambiguity, making her case doubtful because (says he) the modern Church has corrected her stupidities and mistakes.

Furthermore, says this master, just as badgers' skins were followed by rams' skins dyed red and adorned by gold and other embellishments for the covering of Moses' tent, similarly also the plain teaching of the early Holy Church with her simple worship was followed by the much wiser later Church, matured in her rituals and refined in her sacraments, splendid and beautiful.

The original Church was stupid because she worshipped without vestments, without altars, and without church buildings, and knew naught but to say the Lord's Prayer. The present church knows how to honor God because she built great and costly cathedrals and altars out of stone, she ordered rich vestments and blessed everything, she produced many prayers and songs at masses, she honored God bountifully with ornamented churches, walls painted and dressed up with tapestries, with lights, bells, and organs, with singing in high voices, plainsongs, and melodies with polyphonic notes. All this has the wise Church secured for the honor of God! For He yearns so much to be honored; yes, He is sad if there is not enough wax to burn and if the walls do not shine with resplendent colors! This is why he (the Auditor) scorned the stupid Church so much during his lecture. But his new Church has elaborated long rituals for every occasion and sacrament, with proper incantations and benedictions intoned by powerful bishops. And when they are done with all these sacramental invocations they sell the sacraments for money to common people. What a grand way to honor God, indeed, with all these sacraments, with these Simoniacal and sacrilegious customs! The wiser Church decidedly excels the stupid Church in her blasphemous inventions! The blunt-witted Church distributed sacred things foolishly without charge, while the wise Church knows how to strike a profitable bargain with them.

Moreover, says this master, the Original Church was poor. But I say that she was not bad in poor times! From the time of Christ's death to the days of Emperor Constantine, all those who worshipped in the name of Christ lived frugally even though they were greatly tempted by both Jews and Gentiles, so that the name of Christ and his followers was damned by all;

faithful Christians were tortured to death by all other nations. For these happenings, undoubtedly, the original Church was poor and unwise, in a sad estate. The present Church is wise in Christ, while the original Church was foolish and poor for Christ. The matured Church has prospered with riches and with honors of this world; she rests in peace while others carry the sword of temptation for her. Prosperous is she, sweetly singing praises to God in her chapels, reclining behind plenteous tables and on soft couches, prosperous and wise in Christ. You have chosen the better part, until it shall be taken away from you!

Again, says this master, all wise things taught by the present Church – particularly those concerning the temporal power – are based on the teachings and practices of the early apostles. Were this not a lie, truly an enormous number of people would be saved and the glory of God would increase, so rich is the Church in possessions (But God will not accept the offerings of this ugly Church, rich in things displeasing His eye). But to go on, this doctor asserts in his speech that Christ and the Holy Spirit, having established themselves in the Church at Basel, direct through her the salvation of mankind. And, indeed, this is the manner in which the Council calls itself in its documents:

"The Most Holy General Council at Basel, called together by the Holy Spirit, signifies the Catholic Universal Church… Wherefore this Church, governed by the Spirit of truth, having with her the Holy Spirit abiding forever and the presence of Christ until the end of the world…"

If he did not lie, surely this would make a beautiful song! And his Church, possessing the Holy Spirit, is supposed to direct and bring about the salvation of mankind! She is infallible in her judgment, and she could not cease honoring and praising God even if she would, because the Holy Spirit has descended upon her, depositing his treasures in her vestry, intending to establish his good pleasure in her tents more abundantly than in the apostles, for ever and ever. What a lie! Who could be equal in his fabrication and what devil could gloat more shamelessly and wallow in falsehood more impudently than he who opposes and exalts himself against everything that bears the name of God?

91

Let him who can understand, see and behold the signs by which this multitude is encompassed as by a deluge, all this luxury and glory usurped in the name of the Holy Spirit, this domination in his name, this infallible dispensation of salvation, and this presumption that the Holy Spirit is making his eternal abode in the Church! Who dares – from among this befuddled people – to jump over the mountain? They crawl after signs and they are dragging about more sparkling ornaments than the whole half of the open heavens could give, scaring all the drunken people of this earth with their gaudy theatre.

Let him who is humble come and behold the vainglorious haughtiness! For a congregation of fornicators has entered into a covenant with the Holy Spirit and the Holy Spirit reigns over them who are an assembly of harlots, assassins of righteous men, and transgressors of all commandments of God. But he, this shameful nude, refused to put on anything less than the raiment of the Holy Spirit, and he rules over the good things of Christ, not stupidly, but cleverly, in the disguise of the Holy Spirit, and is more generous and wise than the apostles. The devil who dwells among us under a shadow as it were, has a rich accoutrement indeed, and who shall unveil his face that he hides by the shadow of the Holy Spirit?

CHAPTER 14

THE CHURCH LOSES ITS PERFECTION

THROUGH THE DONATION OF CONSTANTINE

All this having been said and done, I shall return to the beginning, that is, to Peter's net, which is the net of faith and with which he has been sent out for the spiritual fishing. (We read of) how he enclosed a multitude of fishes; we also described how that great shoal was organized by the fisher-apostles. And now we shall speak about how it happened that the net, filled with many fishes, began to break.

No one at the time of fishing knew that the net of faith had also enclosed a great number of adverse fishes because they remained quiet in the net for a long time after Peter and other apostles. However, after a certain period of time, when men were sleeping and lulled into security, their enemy came in the night and sowed weeds among the wheat. So when the plants came up and bore grain, then the weeds appeared also.

Where else could this heavy slumber have befallen except here among the priests showered with riches and domains by the Emperor? Those men slept, benumbed by a heavy dream, (intoxicated by their newly won wealth) after a poverty to which they had held by faith. Formerly they preached about the poverty of Christ and his disciples and other faithful priests after them; now they reject poverty having accepted domains, imperial honors, and even precedence over imperial authority. (In their former estate) they accepted poverty as (a part of faith) commanded by Christ and His example. It shows that the priest must have been stunned in dream and have a blackening of his heart to be able to make this quick and easy change: after poverty, to plunge into such luxury and such an exalted position in the world. In the beginning he hid in caves, among rocks and in forests for Christ's name, and behold, now the Emperor guides him around Rome, seating him on a white mare – or was it a white horse? No matter! It always was a 'bird of ill omen' – paying him homage ostentatiously before the whole world. That is the way it was recorded by those who wrote down what they saw for future generations: multitudes in Rome ran to behold that wonder shouting, "Papa, Papa! The Pope! What is it? What goes on? Look there, the Emperor himself saddled the horse and, seating the Priest, he leads him through town!"

Inasmuch as he has done this, it seems to me that he has desecrated the purity and innocence of the apostolic state and that he has not followed properly and sincerely the true faith. Probably he (later) regretted the time when he had to hide in caves and in forests before pagans; for in those days they were killed for the faith in Christ, therefore hiding wherever they could. And that is very hard to the priests of sensuality and comfort of today; they have become accustomed to honors and to physical licentiousness. They could hardly go back to be again the despised of the earth, to administer the legacy of the apostles, to be hunted like dogs and to hide before Constantine. We understand that there are two people in Bohemia who would like to be priests with this burden of the priestly office. But a dissipating and inactive life pleases much better the majority of the priesthood. It was, indeed, very agreeable to Sylvester of a corporeal heart and an incomplete faith to see the Emperor beneath him, leading the horse. In that moment he did not fear him though he was afraid before.

It was then and there that the net became greatly torn, when the two great whales had entered it, that is, the Supreme Priest wielding royal power with honor superior to the Emperor, and the second whale being the Emperor who, with his rule and offices, smuggled pagan power and violence beneath the skin of faith. And when these two monstrous whales began to turn about in the net, they rent it to such an extent that very little of it has remained intact. From these two whales so destructive of Peter's net there were spawned many scheming schools by which that net is also so greatly torn that nothing but tatters and false names remain. They were first of all the hordes of monks in all manner of costumes and diversified colors; these were followed by hordes of university students and hordes of pastors; after them came the unlearned hordes with multiform coats-of - arms, and with them those of the wicked burghers. The whole world and its wretchedness have entered Peter's net of faith with these evil hordes.

And the multitude of these wretched hordes arrogate to themselves pagan and worldly rule, every one of them endeavoring to have dominion over the others. They try to embrace as much of the earth as they are able, using every means and every ruse or violence to get hold of the territory of the weaker, sometimes by money and at other times by inheritance, but always desiring to rule and extend their realm as far as they can. And in order to rule they divide: some are lords spiritual and some are lords temporal. The spiritual lords are the Pope, who is the lord over lords, the lord cardinal, the lord legate, the lord archbishop, the lord patriarch, the lord pastor, the lord abbot, the lord provost (and there are as many abbots and provosts as there are monasteries and orders endowed with estates), the lord provincial, the lord prior, and the lord *magister universitatis*. And the temporal lords are the lord Emperor, the lord king, the lord prince, the lord magnates, the lord burgrave, the lord knight, the lord page, the lord judge, the lord councilors, the lord mayor, and the burghers.

And all these lords draw power to themselves so strenuously that not only have they torn the net between them but they have torn and divided among themselves earthly kingdoms, so that the sovereign, the king, has no one to rule over, nor has he enough income to maintain himself and his retinue. For the ruling abbots have taken over wide areas of land, and the canons and nuns took possession of cities, castles, regions, and villages. And on the other party, the noblemen and their pages, has possessed the remainder, so that in this whole area there isn't in many a mile a single village left for the king to rule over. The country squires would like to have had a foreign king, a rich German, who would add alien countries to his own; for they, having received the king's dominion, will not give it up but would prefer to obtain additional lands from those he has conquered.

It is clear that a royal realm fares better among pagans than among these confused Christians, who have appropriated to themselves dominions. For among the pagans there are no such ecclesiastical lords, so increased in numbers and so useless as sores on a body, for pain is the only thing they give. Really, pagan kings rule much easier since they have no ecclesiastical authority, a nobility richer than royalty and greedy to add kings' possessions to their own domains. Nor had the Jews to contend with such (feudal) domains; there was only one chief lord among them, i.e., the king. There were no peers but only a greater or lesser number of warriors and brave men who the king had at his disposal, making out of them his officials. But the Jewish priests were not supposed to have any temporal power nor inherited land grants, for God granted them only tithes from the people for their livelihood. For these reasons a Gentile or Jewish earthly kingdom could carry on much easier than among these befuddled men who imagine to count something in Christ's eyes, and yet cannot attain to the least pagan justice – they who themselves sprang from the pagans, making themselves into nobility in spite of Christ's intentions!

And, just as temporal government cannot exist properly with too great a number of lords, similarly and more so, Christian faith cannot stand and be preserved with a multitude of wicked hordes and a crowd of lords, so

95

useless and destructive of faith, men who cause division, inequality, haughtiness, oppression, hatred, conflicts, and violence of some against others. Even though they boast of being of one faith, they are far behind the pagans in respect to unity, which is rent by their wicked machinations.

Our faith can encompass a great number of people for salvation, but they all must be of one heart and of one spirit, and nothing is further than that from the divided parties. Their acting is far removed from the spirit of Christ, they are far removed from one another; the people are removed from the lords, who constantly clamor to be promoted in order to have dominion over others, and they are proud as peacocks, which pride is a most abhorrent thing to faith. And all these wicked hordes and multitudinous lords try to be different from one another – and it is with those differences that they measure faith, tearing up Peter's net. These hordes, each one of them being established under different laws and special human justice of their own choosing, behave as if they were superior to and truer than the law of Christ. By this attitude they deviate completely from faith, and in doing so they rend and tear the net of faith.

And as they depart from the law of Christ on account of their own special laws, there results division of one horde against another because every one of them glories in its own laws, regarding them superior to the laws of other hordes; (among the ecclesiastical hordes, for instance) one thinks to be, superior because of its law ordering the wearing of cheap garments, or because they must eat no meat, or because they must not talk, or because they must sing sad tunes, or because they must get up early, or because they must fast a great deal, or because they must keep long matins. These and other details of their laws split these orders, imbuing them with predilection for their own exclusive law and an inclination to disparage, hate, and speak ill of the laws of others. And this contempt breeds dissolution of that unity which faith favors and maintains; by losing true unity they offend and wound faith. All the temporal lords who, begotten by Constantine and established through deception in the name of faith, enjoy pagan ruling and pagan sodomitic living; they put themselves apart from Christ and cannot be partakers of his fellowship; they feel contempt for one another, are prouder than the devil, oppress through power and throttle the weak through violence. All of them offend faith with their destructive particularities, tearing the net in the degree in which they are contrary to faith.

Therefore, when we try to appraise the spiritual situation we cannot compare the body of Christ with the Roman Church, which divides (society) into three groups:

▶ The first group is that of the lords, kings, and princes, who fight, defend, and attack.
▶ The second group is that of spiritual priesthoods who pray.
▶ The third group is the workers in bondage who are supposed to provide for the physical needs of the other two classes.

If the body of Christ is divided by such an order of things, what inequalities are there present! Naturally, this order is agreeable to the first two classes who loaf, gorge, and dissipate themselves. And the burden for this living is shoved onto the shoulders of the third class, which has to pay in suffering for the pleasures of the other two guzzlers – and there are so many of them! When the weather is sultry and hot, pilgrims look for rest under a cool roof, and in the same way they hurry anxiously to become lords. When they cannot be lords, they ask to be at least their lackeys, in order to be, in some way, partakers of their abundant tables and luxuries, getting up and sitting down in emptiness. Yes, the priests too, hurry anxiously to be knighted, and they even like to lackey for the princes because of their overburdened rich tables. It is these two groups of lazy gluttons who, for their own pleasures, drain the working people of their blood, and tread on them contemptuously as if they were dogs.

If this were the true body of Christ or his Church, how improbable the words of Saint Paul would then sound – Saint Paul who speaks of the spiritual body and the different dispositions of its members, a body in which there is no discord and no inequality and in which one member does not oppress another against its will; he says about them:

If one member rejoices, all rejoice together;

97

If one member suffers, all suffer together.

They love one another; if they have something good, they divide equally; if something bitter befalls them, they drink it together comforting one another. But in that three-cornered body, some are sadly weeping while others make fun of them; some sweat in terrible labors while others loiter in pleasant coolness. All these inequalities, so offensive to truth, have been brought about by the sundered wicked hordes. And they forget especially the words that he spoke preparing himself for death and praying for his disciples so that they might remain faithful and for those chosen for salvation. In that prayer he said:

I do not pray for these only (that is, the disciples), but also for those who are to believe in me through their word, that they might all be one; even as you, Father, are in me, and I in you, that they also may be in us, so that the world may believe that you have sent me. The glory that you have given me I have given to them, that they may be one even as we are one: I in them and you in me, that they may become perfectly one.

In that passage it is declared that the people who want to please God and to be saved through the death of Christ – a salvation for which Christ prayed here – must be united in this divine unity and be perfect in it so that all those who believed in him through apostolic preaching until our own day might be one, remaining in the unity in perfection, and in equality. Like members of one body, they, too, must have equality in grace, obedience, mutual help, long-suffering befitting those who have one God, one Lord and Father of all, one faith, and one law for all their doing.

When all are one, the things of God belong to all; otherwise they could not be one, dividing the things which are of God, usurping to themselves special divine rights, and elevating themselves at the expense of others, in violence.

Such a unity we are given in Christ's faith, for our conduct. Anything that deviates from that faith is sin. The above-mentioned hordes, who distinguish themselves from one another by peculiar laws and pagan administration, are not included in Christ's prayer, not one of them, because they are not united with him in his spirit and in his law.

To be sure, the wicked men have entered into all kinds of unions, but Christ's disciples cannot be in them, since these unions cannot bear comparison with the law of Christ, which is based on true honest goodness and in which the people of God are ruled by the truth of his word, in faith and in grace, like the household of one husbandman, standing in true obedience before God aside from whom there is no other lord. There can be no greater unfaithfulness to the rule of God than the division and sundering caused by these factions and their arrogation to themselves of laws apart from His law. The law of God will not assent to their conflicting peculiarities; indeed, every horde tries to draw God down to itself, desiring to have its distinctive peculiarities sanctioned by the law of God. God can sanction only those things that grow out of His law; he cannot approve of anything that grows out of foreign roots. And there is only one law of God, perfect in itself, and so good that all can confirm themselves in it, that they "may become perfectly one" in Christ. This law will bring about an equality of all, they shall love one another as they love themselves, they shall carry each other's burden, and each shall do to others as he wishes that they would do to him.

This commandment could make one multitude out of a thousand worlds – one heart and one soul! There can be no better administration for mankind sojourning in this world; it will lead man into the fullest life, it will make man most precious to God, and man will become a gain to man. Who becomes acquainted with the law of God cannot create nor recognize nor obey any other law, for no other law is right. If there is one right law descended from God, any other law must in fact be contrary. And the contrariness of human laws is made manifest to the law of God by creating multiform hordes under one "faith" (coupled) with superstitions and with the art of differentiation and specialization, with dissensions, with iniquitous thoughts which increase like tares springing up from bad seeds, tarnishing the whole crop. But the law of God is untarnished and enlightening souls. It is so effective and perfect that – no matter what tarnish and sins it finds on men – if men attach themselves to it, believing, it will cleanse them from all sins, maintain them in innocence, and keep them from being overcome by temptations. It can improve or do away with whatever dissenting heretical hordes it finds, that is, he will join them into one people, one faith, one interpretation of the faith, one love, and one hope, if they will only believe the divine law. It will do this to fulfill the things for which our Lord prayed, "that they may be one as we are," as the Father and the Son are one.

The divine law is able to convert a sinful man to God, and to cleanse him from his sins; only the will of God can do this, not human statutes. Man can excel in perfection in accordance with human statutes, but if they have no goodness expected of God in fulfillment of His law, they count for nothing and remain apart from Him and His law. It has pleased God to choose only one perfection, sufficient to all people, and He has not established nor chosen any other laws under which the many hordes could justify their divisions, customs, interpretations, and deeds.

We have spoken about the many hordes, existing under the disguise of faith, that have strayed from the law of God and torn the net of faith, only by lip-service professing their belief, hiding behind sacred symbols of the glory of faith and so completely covered up by them that they appear like Christians when, in fact, they are the domestic enemies of faith and of the chosen ones of God.

CHAPTER 15

THE POPE'S GUILT IN THE TRANSACTION

CALLED "DONATIO CONSTANTINI"

We shall consider every one of the wicked hordes separately, about how they offend the law of God, and in what particular way – distinctive from the techniques of other hordes – they rend the net of faith. But first of all let us look at the two mighty whales which have done the greatest damage to the net of faith and which still keep on tearing it, namely, the chief spiritual lord and the chief earthly lord.

First, consider the spiritual lord, how he has pressed himself into the affairs of this earth and into the pagan play of power, presuming withal to follow the apostolic faith or the apostolic office, while actually desiring to rule over both the world and the faith. This High Priest offended the law of Christ for the first time when he abandoned the honesty and innocence of the apostolic state which he was bound by faith to maintain until death, that is, to remain in poverty and to continue working, preaching, and in any other service appertaining to the apostolic vocation. Therefore, to abandon this laboriousness, simplicity, poverty, and humility is no easy transgression of the law of God and the apostolic state. He could not have offended the divine law and the apostolic state to profoundly had he not at the same time been sitting in the place of the apostles, carrying out their office.

Furthermore, he could not have offended the law of God by giving up simplicity, poverty, humility, and work, had he not been bound to keep these qualities until death by the law of God. To abandon the law of God to do things reprehensible to it – that is, insulting it! We find it clearly written in the Gospel that the apostolic man is bound to poverty, humility and work, in imitation of the example of Christ and his apostles to whom he said, "Follow me, and I will make you fishers of men." They accepted the words of Christ and kept them until their death, not owning any business, estate, or temporal fief. They kept his commandment. Sylvester was duty bound to keep it, too. And he is guilty of transgression because he did not abide by his obligation.

The High Priest has offended the law of Christ and the apostolic office for the second time when he brought distasteful additions into the apostolic state; he thinks to increase the dignity of the apostolic office by accepting imperial domains and worldly honors superior to the Emperor. He is burdened with a monstrous pride, enjoying it when people kneel and fall before him as if he were God, and he is busy with the administration of his domains and with physical pleasures.

And with all this he imagines himself a worthy successor of the apostles when, in truth, he has desecrated his priesthood and corrupted his office by these revolting privileges. The more he holds to things contrary to

101

apostolic teaching, the more he defiles his office in which he calls himself vicar. He has the office but does very little officiating: he seldom celebrates mass, he never preaches, and he never works; that is, the only work which he instituted for himself is the blessing of those he loves and the excommunication of those he does not love. And so he lies in luxuries and gorges himself like a hog wallowing in a sty. It is true that Sylvester himself did not live such a debauched life, but it is he who introduced all this paganism by accepting pagan ways of ruling and worldly emperor-like honors; all that evil he planted in the throne which they call the See of Saint Peter (no one has ever seen Peter sitting on so proud a seat!).

He was grafted by the Emperor onto the tree of pagan rule in order to enjoy the most exalted priesthood, and everything stemming from the grafting of this tree is supposed to be more worthy of respect. Pope Melchiades confesses about the imperial grafting of that See that Constantine, the first Emperor who accepted faith, granted a general permission to all people everywhere in his realm not only to become Christians, but also to build churches and to found church endowments. The same Emperor showered great gifts on the Church and erected the first basilica of Saint Peter. Thus, having left his imperial see, he gave it to Saint Peter and his successors. In this way a deep root was planted, strong and full of poison, and from it grew a bush full of all sorts of poisonous fruits. And the world has been poisoned to death by it.

CHAPTER 16

THE POPE'S GUILT (CONTINUED)

The aforesaid as well as other evidences show clearly that the Highest Priest has been grafted by the Emperor onto the tree of worldly dominion. He has accepted a most exalted priesthood through imperial authority in such a manner that not only did he attach sovereignty to his own person, but also everything else had to stem from his power; no people or nation could have priests except by his authority and sanction. He could disestablish priests, even the best of them, if they dared to speak up against his exalted throne. They must have the same intentions and the same spirit as he, accept churches as he, contribute to his throne in order to remain everywhere in his favor, and exalt his power above that of Christ.

The priest has inflicted an incurable wound on Christ's faith. And the people do not feel his pain; they are dead and insensible to all these damages in which souls perish. That great priest is the fountain from which flows priestly power to all people, and not only priestly power but also even full salvation for all flows from that fountain, (a salvation) contrary to Christ. By the Emperor himself he is counted among the highest princes; the Pope trains his priests to honor him in the same way; (thus) the clergy of Christ is taught in the servitude of a faith stemming from the Emperor and founded on earthly things, which is a faith of an alien spirit, contrary and remote from the spirit of Christ, agreeing instead with the spirit of the Antichrist.

These things enter into the apostolic and Christian faith by the power of the highest priest; who, therefore, dares speak of the corruption of the faith, which is like a great fountain out of which there swims a great horde of obnoxious priests? They are all drawn to titled honors because of temporal benefits and a satiated and empty life and because – being of the nobility – they can evade the labors of those who earn their bread in heavy toil. Those knaves who have ascended to nobility do not bother caring for human souls.

A corpse was added to the churches; and it is only ravens that are drawn to a corpse. Where there ought to be witnesses of Christ's sufferings, there are but Judases who betray Christ, sell His truth, and corrupt the people with the poison of many errors. All this is maintained by and borne of the great priest who has arrogated to himself power over Christians, and who alone through his authority selects priests for them. Who shall dare say that through him faith is corrupted? For everybody can see for himself that there is no more faith; that a villainy planted by Caesar was let loose to kill faith in the world.

Where there was faith before it has been extinguished. Thus the sin of the head has spread into all the members of the body.

CHAPTER 17

THE POPE'S GUILT (CONTINUED)

The third feature with which the great priest has defiled faith and the Savior consists in the fact that with the rich and haughty princely investiture he has arrogated to himself divine power, no, the power of the Savior himself, the power to forgive sins, which is God's prerogative. He alone forgives all people, pardoning their iniquities; and Christ the Son of God died for these iniquities. The witness of faith says that He (Christ) is the Lamb of God who takes away the sin of the world – He alone has the right to forgive the sins of the world because He is both God and man. He died in the fashion of man, for sins, and gave Himself up as a sacrifice to God, on the cross. Through Himself and His pains He has bought forgiveness of sins for the world. Thus He alone has the right and power to forgive sins. Therefore the high priest, exalting himself in his monstrous pride above all that is called God, has seized Christ's prerogative by robbery. And this he manages lucratively, initiating a pilgrimage to Rome from all countries faithful to his banner, and proclaiming to all pilgrims forgiveness of all sins and suspension of punishments. A person may be burdened with the greatest and most evil sins; yet all he has to do is to take them to Rome and he will be made as pure as if he were just newly born! At least this is being said, and the promises are given as it were to fools benumbed by great drinking bouts. And thus large benumbed crowds from all countries stream (to Rome) and he, the father of all evils, gets ready for the ceremony. He puts on white pearled gloves and, standing high (on the balcony), gives his benediction to all the throng, with the forgiveness of all sins and remission of suffering. Whatever post-mortal tortures were supposed to come to them in the purgatory, these are rescinded for those whom he has blessed – he forgives everything! Yes, he has the power to abolish hell as well as purgatory because, when he forgives everybody their sins, there is no one therefore (left) to go to hell. And there is supposedly only one purpose of the purgatory: whoever does not repent enough here for his sins, has to make up the difference by suffering in purgatory in order to satisfy God. The Great Priest forgives all these sufferings – and no one will go to hell or to purgatory.

Now to go further, he not only initiates such lucrative pilgrimages to Rome from all countries, but he even sends to those countries letters containing the forgiveness of sins and sufferings; (he tells them) not to inconvenience themselves with a long journey to him, that he will forgive them everything provided they pay for it in golden ducats; that the sinner is free to specify what sins he wants to have forgiven and that, if he pays for it, he (the Pope) will grant him in a letter a freedom to sin for as many years as are paid for, even until a man's death if so desired. Any priest can absolve all sins at a deathbed by the power of the Pope. And the people buy from that Great Priest their freedom to sin.

These things, therefore, are evident: Christ has the divine right to forgive the sins of the world. Does he have, then, an official in his service to whom he has given his full powers? What is intrinsic to the Lord, the servant has arrogated to himself, usurping also all honors pertaining to his Lord; he increases his wealth in worldly ways, enriching himself by the sale of indulgences and prebends, by endowments and wars; he intrigues with kings and sells indulgences in various countries in order to secure money for his warfare. This was shown in the days when Boniface was at war with the King of Naples; he invoked anathema upon him and with him he excommunicated the whole country so that they could not even bury their dead. Such a disciple of Christ made naught of the teachings of his Master and trampled them in the dust.

Of what use is Christ to us, indeed, if the great priest, his vicar, can forgive all our sins and remit all sufferings, sanctify us, and make us just? What more can Jesus add to this? For it is only our sins that are in the way of our salvation. And if the high priest forgives these, what is left to poor Jesus Christ? Why does the world neglect him and why does it not seek salvation from him? Only because this great priest has overshadowed him with his great pomp and glory received from the world, generously giving salvation in a way in which the world desires it. Wherefore the crucified Jesus is made into a laughing-stock before the world, while only the great priest is on the lips of the world, which in him alone seeks salvation, believing to find it there.

CHAPTER 18

THE POPE'S GUILT (CONCLUSION)

The fourth feature of the great priest with which he has defiled faith consists in the fact that he has greatly increased the number of laws contrary to the law of God and His faith; behind these laws the people have forgotten the true law of God, and they do not even suspect that there exists another faith but that which is presented by the laws of the great priest. All visible worship conducted by the ecclesiastical hordes is done in accordance with his rules. He prescribes the ways and manners of worship, and they are carried out in the sacraments, in religious services, in prayers, and in masses. The Caesarean priesthood is unable to pray or to serve mass otherwise than by mumbling out of the Books of Hours of which there have been written many at his behest. They regard it as prayers when one priest responds to another priest, when they chase one another with words and verses. They bless, fast, and go through rituals and bowings, and all this is done in accordance with the law that the great priest gave them. The people are therefore ignorant of the law of God and have strayed from it; and the Christians have known nothing about it for many centuries. In its ignorance the people take for granted as Christian faith the regulations of the Pope and the practices of worship carried on under the name of God... They have never heard anything else concerning religion excepting (the requirement) to take a glance at God in church and not to plough their field on Sundays; they do not know that there exists any other form...

Therefore, even though these laws are resplendent in a great institution, through religiosity reverence, and respect to God, they are only for form's and feel's sake. But the truth is that there is no middle way here: either deny God and be a dissenter, or cling to Him with your whole heart. Either step is hard to take by the people; for man is not as bad as to want to deny God and relinquish Him; on the other hand you will find very few who want to cling to God with their whole heart. It is this accursed middle way that offers a relaxation to both parties. Fallible and fortuitous are all the advantages hidden in the laws of the Pope who glitters with great orders, outward forms, and ceremonies of worship.

Papal laws are very welcome to those who have never experienced God; they are the means whereby they can cunningly stand in the fold of faith and confess God with their lips only, honor and worship Him only outwardly, and debase their bodies by mortification according to the decrees of the great priest. This brought about an ignorance of God and His laws to such an extent that not even the devil could have invented it. He would not be able to produce a trick whereby men, deprived of their true goodness (consisting of obedience to God's laws), would be made to adhere to a false and fallacious goodness glorying in the laws of the great priest and adorned by divine Scriptures (in order to give the impression that they are being fulfilled – but this is only glorious lying underneath the veneer of letters).

It is obvious how much the laws of the Pope contradict those of God: they assume the coloring of the divine law, lacerating it worse than lion's teeth. Yes, the Pope has greatly defiled the laws of God, by multiplying his own laws contrary to those of God, and even rescinding those of divine origin. He regulates faith for as much as he is its ruler. In Basel his servants have declared concerning the cup of God that the Holy Church can change and abolish the commandment of Christ which says that the common people should drink Christ's blood from the cup; that the Holy Church can abolish what the law (of God) commands as well as pass amendments contrary to it. Being the rulers over faith and God's law, (the churchmen) abolish what they do not like and add what they like, and others must accept what they decide. They keep silent about the fact that many members (of the church) are the worst enemies of the law of God, and men are tortured on that account.

The Emperor, the kings, and the lords have exalted over the Christians this high priest, endowing him with power and domains; now in his pride he rules even over kings. In investing him they were seduced by the proud devil, and through this error they render him service: they raised a lord to the destruction of faith, and now he rules and changes and fabricates laws full of poison and pest, with which to vitiate and wound the people.

The Donation (of Constantine) is no trifling matter: today poison is running in the Holy Church. When the poison was poured into the Church in the beginning, it increased and spread throughout the whole world by means of this wealthy priest, successful in the world, through his corrupt laws. The world became swollen and distended with gross iniquities. Its body became swollen with anger, with prodigality, profligacy, and with a lethargy caused by the loss of life in God; it sneers at all things divine and grows out of the poisons of the great harlot. Thinking of these things, Saint Paul could not have condemned him more than by saying that he was a man of lawlessness and a son of perdition. Christ Jesus the man of virtue came to conquer sins – this man of sin came to multiply it. With all his acts he set the world on the highway of sin, giving it freedom and incentive to sin, easily removing sins from the people by benediction, without repentance, without changing the evil intention, without improving life; he always forgives and the people are not conscious of sinning either before or after. Thus sins are no more sins because human conscience has been separated from sinning; and if there are some who have a sinful conscience, it will be assuaged for money. Thus, he is the Father of Sins, begetting sins with his offices and services and removing the people from the law of God...

This Whale has so torn the net of faith that it has been rendered useless for catching fishes. And if somebody should laboriously mend it in fear and try to 'fish' people unto salvation, he forfeits his neck, for (the Pope) hates the faith which is the net of Peter. That is why he invaded the net; he did not rend it without reason, for it bothered him and harassed him to no end. For, wanting to have a wide way, he sundered the net of faith so that it would not hinder him and his freedom of movement. And he cannot tolerate anyone to fish with the whole net, for, in doing so, the (fisher) would reveal him naked and destroy his work, forasmuch as a complete net would mean shame to his face and death to his pride and luxury. Desiring to continue in his exalted rule and to be given dominions and honors greater than the Emperor, he is bound to make room for himself and to destroy the net; he can endure only its tatters. Where its gaps would reveal his shameful nakedness he mends them with patches...

So, wherever he can fish out some material gain with the net of faith, he uses some rags and tatters, turning masses and other sacraments into money, using the power of the Keys at the highest market price,

excommunicating the innocent and exercising through them his revenge
against those who would dare to 'fish' with the whole net.

CHAPTER 19

THE "DONATION OF CONSTANTINE" –

THE EMPEROR'S GUILT IN THIS TRANSACTION

The second whale that has invaded and enormously torn the net of faith is
the Emperor with his pagan rule and offices with pagan rights and laws.
He is the root of paganism into which Christianity has turned; it is he who
opened the wound from which pours the blood that is spilled among all
Christians – even here – and all blood that shall ever be shed. When he
entered the net of faith with these evils, he despoiled the innocence and
purity of those who were in the net in accordance with the apostolic
establishment.

As mentioned in the beginning, the churches of God converted to the faith
of Christ from the Gentiles and Jews were scattered throughout all
countries and regions, and speaking all the languages of the Gentiles for
over three hundred years. They were abiding only by the will of God and
paid honor only to the gracious laws of Christ's Gospel, without any
addition of either papal or imperial laws, not having among themselves
any kings with sovereign rights. They were servants among the pagans
and their lords, subject to them only corporeally, paying their taxes and
performing other physical services until the days of Constantine.

When Emperor Constantine was received into the fold of faith with his
pagan rule and rights and offices, then the innocence of the true Christians
was saddened and defiled. It was as if ruffians and abductors established
friendship with honest and chaste maidens, got themselves invited into
their house overnight, introducing their own ruffian laws and declaring
that they would protect the maidens' chastity by virtue of their laws. The
honest and chaste maidens would soon be very much disappointed upon

discovering that they could not defend for long – and with great difficulty at that – their purity and faithfulness which they took upon themselves … to keep until death. They could not preserve it among these ruffians who live domestically with them, who rule over them and who can even order them how to preserve to God their purity – very few true maidens would remain there indeed!

It was similar when the Emperor slipped under the skin of faith with his pagan rule, rights, and offices, and obtained full membership rights of participation with the Christians in their faith and in all things pertaining to God. Having been thus united, they shared among themselves: he their Christian things and they his pagan things. Sylvester, who wanted him to join the faith, did not insist that the Emperor give up everything pagan … if he desired to become a Christian; no, instead he was admitted with all that poison among the Christians.

Even though he became a Christian, he still ruled over the pagans, for, although there was a true congregation of Christians in Rome, there were also all kinds of pagans. He held courts and discharged other offices and duties among the pagans, through the authority of compulsion in accordance with pagan right and law. Later he gave freedom to all of them to become Christian if they so desired, with the promise that he would not persecute them as he had before. So, first he came to the Christian religion with pagan rule, offices, and laws, then he continued in that practice, and many others after him, taking part in Christian spiritual matters. And there can be no doubt but that he made them partake of pagan features with which he came to them…

Here is the proof of pagan deeds; let him who wants to read reckon the number of the beast, and seeking he shall find nothing (in the beast) that is of Christ. Concerning Caesar's fusion of faith with paganism it is written: "Today the poison has been poured into the Church of Christ."

CHAPTER 20

THE EMPEROR'S GUILT (CONTINUED)

These imperial and pagan contributions with which he came to the Christians did not become Christianized then or later. Just as his rule was pagan and was of pagan origin then, so it is now. All these foreign additions brought in this manner into the Christian religion are not part of the true faith; they are a deceitful lie, a trap, disguised in letters with which to offend and seduce the people away from God. The Emperor made them partakers of pagan customs; he accepted, by the fact of his becoming a Christian, to rule over the Christians, but he laid upon them the burden of royal authority as if it were an article of faith. And today the Roman Church confirms all this as being the true faith once given to the saints by the apostles.

Here it might be said: but what about the Christians who were in Rome or elsewhere, under the jurisdiction of Constantine in the days when he was still a pagan? Were they not, then, subject to his pagan sovereignty? Were they not carrying the burden of his royal authority? Why should his pagan rule be harmful when he became one of them, a Christian? Or, why should the burden of royal authority be felt as more harmful after his conversion than before?

Of course, this is right, insofar as we speak of royal authority; before, as well as afterwards, they were standing under that authority. As long as they were in his realm or used his utilities and lived among pagans as servants and outcasts offensive to them, they submitted themselves to this pagan power in obedience in all matters of taxation and corporeal services as the apostles had taught them. In such passive submission they would keep the laws of God and also, they would not cause the pagans to be incited against them (which they would if they refused their duty in matters where it was expected of them). However, they never availed themselves of either their laws, offices, courts, or other rights. For their innocence (firmly grounded in them through their Christian faith) stood without accusation or blemish before God and even before the pagans and had no need to be improved upon by the justice of heathen offices or courts. Through the sincerity and truth of their faith, their innocence was made clearly manifest so that it shone in its brilliance much brighter than justice imposed by imperial power and authority; it was as a clear day compared with night. Therefore the Christians, even though under imperial power, did not mix these distinctive marks of paganism in their daily life. But when the Emperor joined the faith, together with pagan rule, statutes, and administration, all these pagan peculiarities were added to the faith and the Christians obeyed them as pertaining to faith. And this caused their corruption. The things for which the early Christians suffered under pagan authority, these same things Christians of today follow as of faith. They are the peculiarities with which Constantine defiled the faith, pagan peculiarities begotten by heathens, he made them part of Christendom. At first these additions were almost unnoticeable, but with the progression of time they devoured the faith of the Christians, and it is faith that is today unnoticeable and lethargic...

Indeed, there is a great difference between the first Christians who, while under pagan rule, remained aloof from their peculiarities (an aloofness for which they sometimes suffered great oppression and even death), and the present Christians who have adopted immoderately the ways of their former lords; today they do not have to suffer for faith any more. They have adopted as faith the way of the lords; they have grown to ignore God and to know nothing of true faith, having respect only for the laws of the greatly multiplied pagan lords.

CHAPTER 21

THE EMPEROR'S GUILT (CONTINUED)

There are so many different kinds of pagan peculiarities ... that it would take too long to dwell on each one of them. But in speaking about some of them (I would like to say a few words) as regards the respect and honor of the chief lord (Emperor) who purports to rule justly and honestly over the Christians, for the sake of their improvement and for good example.

112

(For the Christians should excel, by virtue of their vocation, in their holy intercourse above all Gentiles and Jews).

The corruption of the original honesty was brought about by Constantine and his successors who, desiring to be Christian as well as the most important lords among the fellow Christians, were bound to be honored by the highest divine respect especially by the Christians themselves; at the same time, they stood in their midst with greatest licentiousness and with the utmost contrariness against God, to the profound detriment of faith. (The Emperor) keeps in his company courtiers and servants of a life most depraved and distasteful to a Christian, a life of most wicked thievery dishonest, shameless, and full of haughtiness and cruelty. They want to possess anything upon which their eyes may glance, full of mischief worldly, clever, habitually inventing new costumes (uniforms) and preoccupied by superficial matters, empty-headed, avaricious by habit, of vulgar speech, shameless in their bearing, of a choleric, cocky, and impudent character, holding in derision and despising all people. When we speak about honesty as pertaining to Christians and to the Christian rulers and their servants – what a farce it is! They are really dead corpses, brought by Constantine into the midst of the Christians from the pagans. A corpse can torture to sickness with its stench, and those who smell it will become contaminated with the scandalous inflictions and hurtful woes that have already brought about a great deterioration of morals among the Christians.

And every place is full of these courtly companies that contaminate faith with unreasoning anger far more dangerously than any other evil ensnaring Christians. The courtly companies excel all others by their temptations and evils. And all this has been smuggled into faith with the pagan rule, like an evil smelling corpse, to the great defilement of faith. And yet, the priests and masters exonerate them for all these things … saying, "This is as it should be, in its proper order; the courtiers have to be that way: gay, free, and courteous – but not pious." It must be as their masters command, and they hide themselves behind (their authority).

But we are concerned here about faith which does not depend upon the foolishness of the courtly people, but upon the truth of Christ; we deplore the paganized evil-doers who were brought in and made partakers of faith – they who can truly fellowship with devils only!

CHAPTER 22

THE EMPEROR'S GUILT (CONTINUED)

The second peculiarity with which Constantine defiled the true faith and imitation of God among the first Christians was shown when he joined faith with pagan dominion, assuming power over the Christians when he became one of their members. And I consider this a serious matter. Having become one of them, he did not take into consideration that the condition of the Christians bound them so firmly to obedience to God that they could not deviate in any way from His law, that a Christian must obey God only, not turning to any other law which would only swerve him from the divine statutes and obedience to them. Constantine, who entered the fold of faith, ... subjected the Christians to pagan law and procedure in order that they conduct their affairs in accordance with pagan civil laws (even though they previously conducted these affairs in accordance with divine commandments). Whenever a suit was filed or any other injustice committed, they had to go with their complaints to pagan officials in court in order that the injustices be settled through pagan authority and law.

And they became accustomed not only to that, but they began to seek help from the Emperor whenever injustice was done to them, to protect them and to carry out revenge against the guilty, thus doing a wrong to their property or life. And, having accomplished these things through the power of the Emperor and his officials, they began to give to him their trust, which was due to God alone. And they became as wicked as the pagans, trusting in man and giving him the honor that belongs to God only. Had they trusted solely in God, they would have settled all their differences by His law and suffered injustices rather than returning evil for evil. (Having not this trust) they defend themselves by means of pagan power, securing redress for injustices through trials in courts, thus departing from God and His law. They have become accustomed to this way and now their consciences are not bothered on that account. They have been thus changed by Constantine who, having entered their ranks, partook of their faith and imposed on them their participation in pagan ways. Even today, the priests and masters propound this to the Christians, saying that they should not become lured by a strange teaching. Yet, this in itself is a strange teaching introduced through power.

Therefore, says the Master Adversary, whenever man gives preference to human institutions and statutes rather than to the law of God, he chooses for himself other and foreign gods; whatever man loves, he loves in preference to Christ Jesus, and that is his god. Thus, when man chooses to obey the imperial statutes for the love of his possessions (that is, to regain them or to protect them by the authority of the Emperor and by abandoning the law of Christ) he chooses at the same time a strange god in the form of the Emperor and his law.

This became so commonplace among the Christians that not only are they not conscious of it, but they boldly refuse to listen to or to believe anything that is said against it. And somewhere else the Master Adversary says that there is no doubt that it would become superfluous and useless to obey the imperial and civil laws and statutes if all mankind obeyed the law and rule of love. The farther mankind strays from the gospel of Christ, the more it needs to obey and abide by these imperial and civil laws. It is as if the people were fed by poison, for they accept human statutes as just and reject the law of the gospel of Christ as impractical.

(Wyclif certainly speaks wisely when he says, "there is no doubt..." For if there were many who would correctly abide by the law of love, imperial and civil laws would become superfluous; the law of love would be sufficient... The civil law is, therefore, necessary – as a bitter vinegar, so to speak – for those who transgress the law of love. From sin sprang the necessity of royal offices and civil laws; they are here as punishment for disobeying God. He does not say that this is the proper thing for mankind to do; it is there to support it only, let it (mankind) fall. Having gone astray from God, the people have only their physical life, which is tired and everywhere limping. Unable to stand or walk, they have to lean against these laws. When hurt by injustice they run to authorities with a complaint, and the authority orders a session of the court; both parties are compelled to attend the session and the court hands them the verdict. Punishment meted out by civil laws does not really fit the crime. It only assuages passions in the same way in which a gnawed bone pacifies a dog. If this sinful generation had no laws by which to abide, revenge would kill one party after another without end, until the whole of mankind would perish. But it lives on, tottering and burdened with evil, because it leans against laws.

However, those who live by the laws of love have a healthy and strong spiritual life. In times of iniquity, temptations, and tribulations they can stand firm, suffering injustice and not returning evil for evil. They have no need of judges and courts of appeal to carry them through difficult days of tension.

The Master Adversary says also, it can easily happen to the people nurtured by poison that it will accept as right only human edicts and statutes, rejecting the law of Christ as impractical. That is to say, the confused Christian people have so many imperial, civil, and pagan statutes and laws that they have become (saturated) with them as with poison. The true inner life perishes after the use of this poison and strays from God and His grace. They have become accustomed to eat and drink this poison in all human institutions and laws, and having been fattened by this poisonous food of errors, they intend to stick to these laws as if they were just or given by God, and to profit temporal gains in glory. For in doing this they enjoy their freedom of will and body, eschewing the tribulations of the cross of Christ, defending themselves at courts, not abstaining from corporeal goods, and being free to mete out revenge and to return evil for evil. He who feeds on this poison enjoys freedom in evil things and can say nothing about such a pagan order except that it is good and just.

It is no wonder that people poisoned by this venomous food defile and reject the gospel of Christ as impractical. On the contrary, his law saddens and disturbs them while the poisonous law pleases them. The law of the gospel requires that they suffer blows on the cheek and that, if anyone should sue them and take their coat, they let him have their cloak as well, thus adding self-injury to injury. Therefore, the people living on a diet of

116

poison – which has been poured also into the Holy Church – corrupt Christ's law with the saliva of garlic and insult from the wise magistrates; their civil service wisdom smells like garlic eaten after a fast – they know how wisely to defame the simplicity of the gospel of Christ, sufficient and vigorous.

Well then, to return to where we began, what do we say about the Emperor entering faith with pagan rule, statutes, and offices? It is clear that – as has then been said – this is *"the poison which is poured today into the Holy Church."* It was not poured in without purpose, but that all people drink it, that all countries and nations be poisoned to death with this corporeal and worldly wisdom. And this wisdom is the foundation of the power of the Emperor and his laws; and drinking this poison through his laws (the people) turn their whole mind to caring about comfort, licentious freedom, temporal goods, to obtaining these things through cunning, to increasing their profits through weal or woe, and to gaining privileges from kings or to winning these privileges back if lost. For all this they invent clever defenses and fortifications for warfare…

This law has converted Christians into pagans. And now, satiated with the poison of the worldly and physical wisdom, they despise the law of Christ. They consider it a ridiculous foolishness that only exposes their fat bellies. And so they not only scorn it as useless, but also are even ready to oppose any one who dares to parade the uncomfortable law of Christ before their noses. You would think it were arsenic!

The poison of worldly wisdom is best revealed in that it leaves people wounded and turned away from God, hateful and scheming how to rise up against truth. They whose veins are filled with the earthly poison consider truth their worst enemy… Yes, when the Emperor joined Christian faith with pagan lordship, he has planted a seed that grew and bore multitudes of transgressors, who prospered and produced such a terrible number of evils that not even the devil himself could invent them all. All these wicked and pious hordes, coated with a veneer of specious holiness have so discredited faith that very few are willing to follow it. They turned the rest of the crowd to paganism.

117

Only what has been planted can sprout and grow. The Emperor has been planted with his authority into the Christian soil. He grew strongly and, having grown, blossomed and produced seed that, planted, multiplied and spread paganism everywhere with its authority, laws, and administration. For, it being in the nature of paganism to deny all faith and all the gospel of Christ, and to ridicule it, authority is of necessity driven back to check it cruelly, while it prospers on arrogant pride, and on godless villainy without comparison. Authority is necessarily driven to check it (the Gospel) cruelly, to torture, to tear, to plunder, to imprison ... and all this in order to tame the uncircumcised mind of the evil-doers and to put them in their proper place.

This course is not the way of faith and salvation; it is good only for the taming of unjust people in their physical lives and temporal goods and for preventing their fall and end on account of their excessive stupidity and temper.

CHAPTER 23

THE EMPEROR'S GUILT (CONCLUSION)

The third feature with which the Emperor has defiled the faith of the followers of Christ ... (consists in the fact) that he uses pagan power arbitrarily and willfully, with plenty of haughtiness and arrogance, paying no heed to the circumstance that he is a Christian and that he uses authority over Christians who were redeemed by the blood of Christ and who are, therefore, servants subject to the authority of the highest Lord of lords; the Emperor himself wants to rule over them, to dictate to them, and to administer them. O, the arrogant pride of the emperors, kings, and other lords! If they would ever remember (that they are Christians) they should never dare rule over people so willfully, just to suit their whims. They would respect and stand in awe before the Lord of this people... They would know that if they rule willfully in whatever manner over the people, against the Highest Lord, they and their rule would fall under His judgment...

I am not too much concerned about the corporeal wrongdoings that they inflict upon the people, such as the collecting of taxes and the imposition of week work and boon work. These corporeal servitudes are the cause of impoverishment and of a fatiguing burden on their serfdom; still, if the people endured them in humility, these (impositions) would not harm their consciences.

However, a much greater concern should be given to the fact that this power and system is so vicious and devoid of good when judged from the point of view of faith. In this matter the lords want to do nothing regarding their consciences or the consciences of those over whom they rule. They are all Christian and at least some of them have, on account of faith, a bad conscience when they kill, do violence to others, and rob them of their property. But (on the whole) they do not hold these things to be sinful. Driven by pride they fight for goods and chattels, for worldly honor, and if someone touches their property, immediately they declare war, round up the people like cattle, and drive them to war where all murder and rob one another. How can it not be dangerous, therefore, for good Christians to live under such powers, which force them to do evil and to trespass the divine commandments! And what I esteem more cruel, they drive Christian men to war – and there are Christians on both sides – with orders to kill and rob others. A brother will go against a brother to do violence to him; he who by faith should lay down his life for him goes to kill and despoil his brother, simply because he is compelled to do so by the ignoble authority. He does not have so much sense or love as to be willing to be killed by his overlord rather than to commit such an evil thing. An arrogant authority is, indeed, a trap for good Christians; it compels its subjects to go and do every evil it can think of.

But the greatest iniquity and crime which the authority has committed, running into the worst form of pagan hypocrisy is revealed when – already so contrary to Christ as it is – it even kills righteous Christians for their faith, spilling their blood. For the apostles of the Antichrist have wound themselves around the heart of authority and use it now to their own advantage and for their own purposes. They have betrayed true Christianity to the powers-that-be, defaming it with heresy. And authority which of itself does not know what faith is, likewise knows not heresy.

But spiritual hounds who hate the servants of Christ and of his law whisper their insinuations into the ear of authority, inciting it to exterminate those heresies with a pious ruthlessness.

That authority is therefore the strength of the Antichrist aimed at Christ and his chosen ones. And the Antichrist, with all his hatred and secret guiles, could not press so hard against Christ, if he had not a great ally in the strong temporal power. To what end has grown this authority, which has branched out its roots (planted by Constantine) among the Christians? It has brought about everything that is abominable to Christ, all sorrows, and all temptations to his saints. The hatred of the Antichrist is incited to flaming anger against Christ and his followers and it strikes the chosen ones of Christ through temporal authority (which authority the Antichrist praises to high heaven saying that through it the Holy Church stands in its firmness and goodness).

CHAPTER 24

THE EARLY CHURCH & THE MEDIEVAL CHURCH

[In this chapter Chelčický refutes the argument which says that the Church can maintain its strength only in connection and with the support of the state authority. And this is the way he proposes to handle the argument:]

What will be discussed here is not easy but difficult, complicated, and painful. Therefore, (I propose) to conduct the arguments in the manner of a disputation between persons of opposing ideas. One will be from the following of Jesus, namely Paul who is a good speaker and well-trained in disputation, and the other will be from the servants of the Antichrist, namely the Simoniacal priest who is the vicar of Judas.

[The whole of this chapter is given to the argument of the Simoniacal priest who maintains that the early Christians of pre-Constantinian times were living in a very unenviable situation, being poor servants, mistreated by their lords, tortured, and killed.]

It is ridiculous therefore to say that the original Church of Christ was in a perfect condition in the days of the apostles and other disciples... On the contrary, the Church of Christ became perfect when it accepted temporal power from the Emperor.

[Paul answers saying that it is wrong to measure the perfection of the Church of God by the standards of perfection of temporal authority.]

For the priest, this was like drinking sour wine from a goblet.

[Paul goes on to say that in gaining temporal security, the Church lost spiritual perfection.]

The lovers of the world repose under the shadow of the authoritarian Church, and secular power protects those things that they love. And in doing this, they build not on a rock, but on earthly considerations weak as sand.

CHAPTER 25

THE EARLY CHURCH & THE MEDIEVAL CHURCH (CONCLUSION)

[Paul continues his argument admitting that the Christians were very poor and living in unpleasant conditions during the first three hundred years but this does not imply that the Church was not spiritually perfect.]

The states and powers are always earthly and temporal. But Jesus declared that he was not a ruler of a temporal kingdom. That is why he said, "My kingdom is not of this world." And he explained this even more clearly to his disciples when he said, "The kings of the Gentiles exercise lordship over them… But not so with you." That means that the dignity of the Church of Christ does not depend on the success of temporal things.

[On the contrary, adversity causes the Church to prosper spiritually; in giving the Beatitudes, Jesus taught his disciples to lose earthly attachments and to cling to things eternal.]

With these speeches Paul describes the fullness and perfection of the original Church, richer in poverty, in patience, and in other spiritual matters than the later Church… It is evident from this disputation that to the big-bellied priest the early Church has a bad odor, it being so poor, with torn sides and a wounded head. Of course, the later Church is safe, peaceful, and protected by the shadow of the Emperor's sword, having learned apostolic men of pink faces, with long tunics and tall miters; here is the heart of the priest brought up in a cool shade! The early Church was rich in spiritual treasures and victorious in many martyrdoms… The Church of Christ is bound to carry its cross and to overcome with patience every injustice until the Day of Judgment.

[Every time the Church has shown impatience or dissatisfaction with its poor condition it has transgressed the commandment of God and committed a mortal sin.]

Therefore, as I have said, the hatred and cruelty of the pagan princes against the early Church was the real reason of the Church's goodness and honesty; compelled by their cruel hatred it was bound to overcome all evil occurrences victoriously in patience, in order to please God, and to fulfill His will by suffering iniquity in adverse times.

CHAPTER 26

STATE AUTHORITY IS OUTSIDE THE MORAL LAW

[The Church, having lost the capacity for patience and long-suffering, has also lost God. Authority based on compulsion and the love of Christ are incompatible terms. The state sovereignty does not admit the possibility of standing under the moral judgment of God. <u>But he who obeys God needs no other authority.</u> "Love does no wrong to a neighbor; therefore love is the fulfilling of the law."]

For the deeds of faith consist in loving God and one's neighbor, and the fullness of the law is love; the secular authority cannot produce this love by its sword, but it descends from above from the Father of Lights into the hearts of good will to whom it is a delight to love God, to do His will, and to obey His commandments.

Judge for yourself, how can state authority approach those who are bound by the divine commandment not to resist evil in times of adversity, but to offer the cheek when the one is struck, to leave revenge to God and not to return evil for evil, to love their enemies and to do good to them, to give them food and drink when they are hungry and thirsty, and to pray for them to God? These are the acts of our faith and these are the commandments of God. So, what can the state authority do about that position? The state authority, therefore, because of its reliance on cruel compulsion, cannot direct a life of obedience to God. A certain tool cannot be used in every trade but each trade has to use its own suitable tools; a blacksmith cannot hold a horseshoe in the fire with a spindle and a woman cannot spin with a pair of pliers. Therefore, pliers are appropriate to the blacksmith and a spindle to the woman.

Similarly, the authority of the state is suited for other things than the Church of Christ. [It is doing good in so far as it restrains the evil-doers.]

CHAPTER 27

THE ORIGIN OF STATE SOVEREIGNTY

[However, in restraining the evil-doers the state has to resort to the evil-doers' technique, which is bad and un-Christian. Those who work for the sovereignty of the state are not without sin. The Christians should have nothing in common with the pagans and the pagans nothing in common

123

with the Christians except for living together. The pagans depend on outward authority, while the Christians depend on the goodness and love that come from the inner life. Chelčický finds this authority of the 'inner man' even in the Old Testament.]

The Jews, having been brought into the Promised Land, lived safely under the protection of God and His laws, living in perfect freedom and having no temporal lord with authority to rule over them and no one to whom they were obliged to pay taxes. And they remained in this freedom for four hundred years, as can be found in the Scriptures. But later, through Satan's insinuations and through their own sins – having rejected their Lord God and His protection – they begged Samuel for a king saying:

"Set up for us a king that may judge us like all the nations around us!" But the thing was evil in the eye of Samuel who spoke of these things to the Lord. And the Lord said to Samuel, "Listen to the voice of the people according to all that they say to you; for they have not rejected you but me from being king over them. Like all the deeds that they have done to me from the day I have brought them up from Egypt even to this day, inasmuch as they have forsaken me and served other gods, so they are also doing to you. Now, therefore, listen to their utterance, and give them a pagan king."

Having asked for a pagan king, they committed a great sin. The Lord sent thunder and rain that day, and the Jewish people said,"We have added to all our sins the wickedness of asking for ourselves a king."

[In asking for a temporal ruler, the Jews scorned God and His law. Just as they rejected divine order by inviting a king to rule over them, similarly also the Christians rejected God by accepting the Donation of Constantine. Before, Christ had specifically set his people apart from pagan authority, not geographically, but spiritually] by purity and innocence, setting the Church apart as a pure bride to be betrothed to her one husband, Christ. They belonged no more to themselves but to him who died for them.

[It was only in that perfect separation from the evil world of temporal affairs that it was possible for the "dwelling of God to be with men."]

What the Emperor could not accomplish by tortures he obtained by favors and gifts; he joined their faith only to drag it into the unfaith of his paganism.

[Emperor Constantine and Pope Sylvester are accomplices in a great conspiracy against God. But this would not be so bad as the fact that they declared their transaction to be of divine sanction. The alliance of Church and state was declared to be in accordance with the true faith, and whoever now dares challenge it is condemned as a heretic.]

CHAPTER 28

WYCLIF'S THREE TYPES OF GOVERNMENT

[This chapter contains Chelčický's commentary on Wyclif's theory that there are three types of government, namely, divine, human, and angelic, and that every Christian has an authority, not civil, but evangelical. The prophets had such authority, and such have the Christian prelates. Pagan kings exercise temporal authority through civil laws and spiritual kings through the law of the Gospel. Commenting on this dualism, Chelčický says:]

Do not mix poison with honey: for the poison, even though mixed with sweets, will not turn into medicine but will always remain poison. Poison can do naught else but kill human beings.

[Therefore, do not drink Antichrist's poison offered to you by Caesar, but abide only by the apostolic honey.] The Pope, too, has mixed poison with Christ's gospel. The foolish person, being attracted to it, cannot escape its venom; he will drink it like gospel. And now therefore, since they have mixed so much poison with the gospel, they can offer much more for drinking than they had before. Thus, under the name of Jesus, they can bring the whole world into paganism. Indeed, in his name they feed the world with poison...

CHAPTER 29

THE ORIGIN OF CHURCH AUTHORITY

[This chapter deals with the rule and administration of 'King Jesus, contrary to the rule of kings and countries.' He is responsible to God only and dependent from Him. This was foretold to Mary by the angel of the Annunciation:]

And you shall call his name Jesus. He will be great and will be called the Son of the Most High, the Lord God will give to him the throne of his father David, and he will reign over the House of Jacob forever, and of His kingdom there will be no end.

[His rule was foretold even in the Old Testament:]

"He shall be ruler over Israel."

When Pilate asked him, "Are you the Jewish king?" Jesus answered by saying, "As you say, I am a king. It was for this that I was born and for this that I came to the world, to give testimony to truth. Everyone who is on the side of truth listens to my voice."

[Jesus is therefore the true ruler of the Christians, and he shows his power by overcoming the ruses of the devil, by releasing the captives from the prisons and all iniquities of the world. And, since everything that man hopes for, everything that a Christian finds valuable in this life, is to be found in the Kingdom of Jesus, man can give his true allegiance to no one but Christ. Chelčický compares the temporal kingdoms of princes and the spiritual kingdom of Christ, and exclaims:]

O, how small and barren are the dominions of pagan kings compared to the dominion of Christ! The temporal power heaps burdens and sufferings upon its subjects instead of freedom and consolation. And yet, the Kingdom of Christ is so powerful and perfect that, if the whole world wanted him for king, it would have peace and all things would work together for good. And there would be no need of temporal rulers, for all and sundry would stand by grace and truth. The need of kings arises indeed, because of sins and sinners... But if King Jesus ruled, all evil would fall away.

[A temporal state rules by force and compulsion; the Kingdom of Christ rules] by free will so that every one may choose of his own accord to leave the way of sin for the love of (Christ) the King, to be ruled by him inwardly. Therefore, if one, two, or more are willing to submit to hi dominion, they must first abandon sin... The beginning of his kingdom is at the end of men's sins... But if his kingdom is defiled, evils immediately spread and multiply. This immediately evokes the necessity of temporal kingdoms to punish excessive sins by the arm of their authority... And they punish with revenge and without charity... The end of Christ's kingdom is salvation; the beginning of earthly rule is perdition. This is what happened to the rebellious Jews who in their pride chose to obey a man king – and how terribly they had to suffer! It is to their punishment that God says:

I am your destruction, O Israel; who can help you? Where is your king now, that he may deliver you, and all your princes that they may rule you of whom you said, "Give me a king and princes"? I gave you a king in my anger, and I took him away in my wrath.

Because of their sins he made their land a waste and a horror ... and made them prisoners of the King of Babylon for seventy years. [The earthly rulers and the state authorities are the punishment of God for disobeying His laws. Good kings may improve the subjects' physical well being and the Christians can grow in their faith; if the kings are bad, the Christians must suffer their iniquities for the sake of salvation. But in either case, neither the good nor the bad rulers can really help the people who are bad. Only they can be saved who are ruled by King Christ the Crucified.] And

127

it will help no one even if St. Peter should rule over him in the fashion of temporal kings. [Wise people therefore seek naught but to serve King Jesus, and they shall prosper in his courts.]

CHAPTER 30

THE DIVIDING LINE BETWEEN THE SPIRITUAL AND SECULAR

[The real difficulty arises from the fact that present day Christians do not know where to draw the dividing line between their faith and the state. They enjoy the protection of the state and share in its advantages. Particularly the clergy and the learned doctors seem to have become allies of the state. In order to make their compromise more plausible they have divided all mankind into three estates] namely:

- ▶ The estate of the ruling class, which conducts defensive warfare, kills, burns, and hangs.
- ▶ The estate of priests who pray.
- ▶ The estate of the common peasants who must slave and feed the two upper-class insatiable Baals.

Behold the first Baal, fat and proliferated: the temporal lords. Behold the second Baal, also fat and proliferated: the spiritual lords. Both Baals suck the labor of the earth, the blood, and the sweat of the third class that, drenched with sweat, fills the fleshpots of the two Baals.

[But the religion of Jesus does not approve of this system. When the rule of Jesus was foretold by the angel, the House of Jacob meant the Church of the righteous, the sheep of Christ who hear his voice:]

"Everyone who is of the truth hears my voice." And again, "My sheep hear my voice, and I know them, and they follow me."

128

Therefore he cannot rule over stinking goats (*sic*), that is, straying Christians, because they do not listen to his voice [but rather obey the authority of the combined Church and state.]

The world is unable to follow his (Christ's) rule for its excellent perfection; for nowhere can man be governed both in matters which pertain to God and in matters which pertain to men, with such benefit for his soul as well as body, as in the sovereignty of King Jesus. We can confess these things by the (assurance of) faith. The royal government has no similarity with the government of King Jesus. A good Christian lives by faith and follows Christ in works; but, as mentioned before, according to the doctors such a Christian should be king with a pagan exercise of power over his sheep; however, it is impossible to reconcile their utterances with the fact that they have ignored King Jesus and his fullness who is the head of the Holy Church. The Church's authority and sufficiency is derived from this head and is (channeled) to all the members (of the body). The doctors have forgotten these things if they are of the opinion that they can obtain a good Christian king with pagan (un-Christian) rule, and through his authority to gain benefits … for the Holy Church. This (division) may suit the Roman Church, which seeks the support of the royal power; its king may defend her, drive away her enemies, and fight terribly with her foes… Indeed, the Church of Rome rather likes a wicked king, for this man – if sufficiently intoxicated by her poisons – will fight for her better than a humble Christian. For a good Christian does not dare to get involved in pagan administration, either to work in the capacity of a king and to do administrative work or to defend (by virtue of his office) the Church of Christ against enemies; a good Christian knows (all too well) that King Jesus wants a different Church from the one which spills blood in his name… A true Christian can do no such thing.

First of all, he cannot do it because he has no reason for such behavior. Secondly, he cannot do it since he has no right to do anything for which he has no power. Thirdly, he cannot do it because his conscience will not allow him to commit anything that might bring about much evil or even do away with much that is good. Finally, he cannot do it for conscience's sake and for fear of offending God.

[A true Christian cannot work or associate with any state office; to do so would mean to condone the violent system of authority that is repugnant to Christ. In addition, sovereignty leads to war.]

Humanly speaking ... wars begin when one lord who rules over people wants to extend his authority over the people of another lord. (Of course) an even greater conflict arises when someone of the king's household tries to usurp the kingship for himself by conspiracy. Absalom was killed for such an action because, having won for himself the favor of the Jewish people, he desired to remove his father from his throne and rule in his stead. How much more, then, is a Christian bound by fealty to his Lord and King Christ Jesus! [Not to be faithful to Christ, that is, to compromise with the state, is tantamount to Absalom's infidelity to David. Absalom was punished by death, and Christians will also be punished if they get entangled with secular power.] This power, with all its offices and officialdom, is contrary to the rule of Christ. Therefore, no honest Christian can have any share in its administration... A faithful servant of Christ ... who would want to admonish the followers of Christ in faith and to urge them not to accept any offices from the king would himself have to avoid being a ruler over the people of his Lord, for this would involve pagan rule and compulsion through power in accordance with the ways of the heathens, that is, the people would have laws contrary to the law of Christ the King Jesus.

CHAPTER 31

THE LAW OF MEN AND THE PERFECT LAW OF CHRIST

The Master Adversary speaks in great detail about the division of civil administration into a secular authority and the authority of the gospel of Christ Jesus.

First of all, the contrariness of civil authority to the law of King Jesus – which is his gospel – is revealed in that God had originally established it, but His firstborn Son has introduced (his) authority for his chosen people,

130

rejecting all other authority. On the other hand, pagan administration bases its own authority on a fiction or imagination of blind sinners who invented laws in accordance with earthly wisdom ... intending thus, by means of power, to subject many to these laws. God has therefore repudiated such a course as sick, deficient, and even unjust... But He has left that law of blind sinners for the pagans who might thus be somehow enabled to live a physical life, in the way of a sick person who, hardly able to toddle, has to lean on a crutch.

The law of God must be held therefore in great reverence... And every man ought to be satisfied with this law for his conduct in this world having no need of mixing it with other laws. Neither God nor Christ require of man anything but to do right. Therefore Christ who is both true God and true man, in whom is fullness and perfection, requires nothing of man but love, and the means to attain to it. And the means are powerfully carried by the law of Christ who taught man in the most masterful fashion how to please God in everything he does... And speaking of the perfection of his instruction, man is not only taught fully what to do Christ's law will enable him to know even those things which would deviate him from true goodness. For no sin can be committed except when we ask those things which Christ condemned, or when we run away from that which he took upon himself to bear. (And we can see this because his whole life on earth as man is an example and a lesson for (our own) behavior... Clearly, he taught most powerfully and most fully ... how to avoid injustice and do good... No law can be more perfect than the law of Christ.

Therefore, a faithful Christian who realizes the powerful strength and perfection of the law of God ... cannot become a ruler with un-Christian authority which had been culled by blind sinners, in fear lest he defile the rule of God with the rule of blind sinners, a rule by which pagans live their life so laboriously.

CHAPTER 32

THE LAW OF MEN AND THE LAW OF CHRIST (CONTINUED)

Now concerning the second difference between the rule of the law of Christ and the pagan rule, the Master Adversary says that the civil or state law of the pagans is (real) law by virtue of the sinfulness of men and for the purpose of obtaining justice through compulsion, while the law of the holy gospel exists for the (sole) purpose of obtaining spiritual gifts of grace... [Civil law administers justice through compulsion, while the law of Christ establishes justice through love.]

[But while law checks – to a certain degree – injustice within one's own country, it does nothing when iniquities are committed abroad.] The straying Christians like to depend on secular power; they even seek it and cherish it since it serves their inclinations... Thus a material-minded people asks to have secular power (over them) because it enables them to rest in peace around fleshpots, under the protection of (state) authority; and if, peradventure, some hardship or threat to life or property should come about, these things will be defended by authority of the king, through war, driving away the disturber, and revenge... [These Christians who have strayed from the law of Christ and are under the jurisdiction of the civil law are regarded as just and good as long as they live up to the standards of the civil courts and offices. But righteousness by law has nothing in common with righteousness in the eyes of God.] The truth of Jesus is nothing but foolishness to proud men, an oddity, an offense, a pain, and a shame.

Here it is necessary to ask: in what consists the superiority of the law of Christ over pagan civil laws? In this, that a (Christian) man adjusts his conduct in accordance with his conscience ... keeping in mind the grace of God and the reward of salvation ... while a subject of the state adjusts his conduct in accordance with the advantageous protection of his temporal legal honor and property. A pagan fights to protect his rights and his property in court or in field; a Christian conducts his life with love, patiently enduring injustice, as he will be rewarded by an eternal gain...

132

He refuses to have any dealings with commercial enterprises and with any profitable speculations, lest he harm his soul… And this is foolishness to the pagan (world).

CHAPTER 33

THE LAW OF MEN AND THE LAW OF CHRIST (CONTINUED)

[Evil has a tendency to perpetuate itself and to grow. The Christians, having fallen away from the way of perfection, keep on falling deeper and deeper. The government of kings and of civil laws only helps in this falling. For even though the civil law seems to check evil, it encourages a continuing fall of man.] It still does perpetuate lawsuits, punishments, and revenge; it returns evil for evil, perpetuates falsehoods, taxes patience, … and in all these matters it is an accomplice of the fall, departing farther and farther from the original state of innocence.

[Speaking of the general state of this 'fallenness' Chelčický suggests that there is only one antidote: utter obedience to the law of Christ.] His law alone can check the fall. The 'fallenness' of man is the root of evil death from which all mortal things are growing: addiction to do evil, possessiveness, anger, hatred, and avarice… And knowing that our old self was crucified with our sins … man can be rescued through his obedience to the laws of Christ. [By persecuting, the evil of the civil law grows; by being persecuted, the innocence of the true Christian grows] and with it, his life of grace.

CHAPTER 34

THE LAW OF MEN AND THE LAW OF CHRIST (CONTINUED)

The third peculiarity with which the civil law and the administration of pagan kings compares unfavorably with the law of the gospel consists in the fact that civil law and rulers compel against the people's will.

The temporal power is called sovereignty because it has the authority to enforce; even when it desires (the common) good without which the world could not stand together, it does so by compulsion. The temporal authority can do so only because the sovereignty of God suffers it in order to keep the world together. If God should desire it, he could wipe out the whole world on account of its iniquity – and all the kings of the earth (put together) with their combined sovereignties could not prevent it! Therefore Jesus Christ, who is the sovereign of his people, requires from them the sovereignty of goodness. And his sovereign goodness is so perfect that he does not even compel his people to be good. Does he not say,If any man wants to come after me, let him deny himself, take up his cross, and follow me?

And if your physical will does not want it and rebels against it, compel it yourself, deny yourself. You yourself must rebel against your unwilling will and follow reason. Cling to God through grace, fulfill His good will by emptying your own ill will for the love of God your Lord! No one can be a follower of Lord Jesus unless he becomes one by his own volition. If one is filled by unwillingness, let him break it and resist it. If he does not break his ill will and tame his will, who else shall do it for him? Does not God say, "Under you shall be your desire and you shall rule over it"?

Christ's dominion is perfect ... and therefore it never uses compulsion... The virtue that he expects from every (Christian) ... springs from a good and free will; originating in freedom, it has (the responsibility) of choice, to choose either the best good or the worst evil. Both these choices stand before man. The Lord Jesus calls us to the best good, the devil and the world call us to the worst evil. Therefore, choose joy or hell. The choice for either of these (ways) is in your hands.

Christ's dominion leads to perfect goodness [and they that follow him follow a king whose rule was ushered in with the words,]

Peace on earth through Jesus Christ, goodwill toward all men!

They who submit to the will of Jesus Christ and to his ... sweet truth ... will have peace on earth through him and no one else... They shall be like sheep following his voice; they hear him and he will give them eternal life. And nobody will take them from his hands, for they hear and know his voice ... and live in his perfection, rejoicing that they are counted worthy to suffer dishonor for his name. Even the Scripture gives this interpretation when it says,The sons of wisdom are the congregation of the righteous, and their mark is obedience and love.

They, the sons of wisdom ... who trust in him will understand the truth, and, faithfully clinging to him in love, they will gladly do his will.

[How different is the secular authority with its compulsion and force!] Therefore a faithful Christian who is a servant of Christ and of his perfect rule cannot be a king with un-Christian authority and with rights contrary to the law of Christ ... lest he pollute the blessed ferment of the wine with stinking poison...

CHAPTER 35

THE LAW OF MEN AND THE LAW OF CHRIST (CONTINUED)

Fourthly ... no true Christian can become a ruler over a people whose true king is Christ. [A true Christian can have no other sentiments but those of equality with others; any action that would spoil the brotherly relation is un-Christian.] He must keep a brotherly equality with all and everybody, love his neighbor as himself, and do nothing from selfishness or conceit, but in humility count others better than himself. How could he be a king if the gospel prescribes to "bear one another's burdens, and so fulfill the law of Christ"?

It is shown in the example of Solomon ... that the burden of rulership is difficult. When he died and his son was about to become king, the Jewish people came to him asking him to be kind and to lighten the heavy burden that his father had imposed upon them. And he, taking counsel with fools, and being a fool himself, answered the people saying, "My little finger is thicker than my father's loins! In other words, he would burden the people more than his father. Because of this foolish answer, ten tribes left him. All this shows that even Solomon, with all his wisdom, burdened his people with great oppression.

Therefore, a good Christian who is obliged to carry his neighbor's burdens cannot impose the pagan burden of authority on others. One day, when the Disciples of Christ disputed who was the greatest of them, Jesus said to them, "Do you know that the kings of the Gentiles exercise lordship over the people, seeking authority, honors, and enrichment?" And they call it a good thing! Therefore Jesus forbids his disciples all lordship with its pride and cruelty and compulsion... "Do you want to be like them? You do not know what you ask for. But not so with you; rather let the greatest among you become as the least."

Such pagan lordship does not befit the people of Jesus, which ought to stand together in an equality of a fellowship of love, and whose ruler is King Jesus. This has been confirmed by that faithful Jew of the Old Testament, Gideon. He, after winning a great victory over his pagan enemies, was asked by the liberated Jews to become their king. But he answered them saying, "I will not rule over you, nor shall my sons rule over you, since God the Lord rules over you." Behold the nobility of this honest man who realized ... that God alone should be their king. [All this proves that the exercise of authority is not becoming a Christian.]

136

CHAPTER 36

THE LAW OF MEN AND THE LAW OF CHRIST (CONTINUED)

The fifth objection against a good Christian's participation in government is this: ... He cannot be king even over evil men ... that is, the Christians who have strayed from ... the path of perfection. No matter how good the intention of a Christian ruler would be, [the result would always be bad and the man himself would get involved in the snares of evil.] A good king ... must abide by a law that he orders ... his people to obey. There exists no king who could rule without having some law... A good Christian who would intend to be a king over an evil people for the purpose of their improvement, could have no better law for this end than the divine law... [In other words, this divine law would make human laws as well as his rule superfluous.]

And what if he who purports to be a king for (the purpose of) betterment of evil people takes the Old Testament for his (law)? And it is a good law since God Himself gave it to His chosen people. The Jewish kings ... led people to do good even by coercion. They were even allowed to war in accordance with this law... But a Christian cannot obey this law because Christ is the end of the Jewish law for the justification of the believers. (In this way we must understand) Saint Paul when he says, If you receive circumcision according to law, Christ will be of no advantage to you. You are severed from Christ; you have fallen away from grace.

... Being circumcised, that is, being bound by obedience to the Law, they could war, murder, steal and otherwise shed blood, all in accordance with the Law; but obeying this Law leads not to salvation in Christ. Thus, a true Christian desiring to be a king could not abide by the old Jewish Law in order to improve evil men. If he really desires to make his people better, he can do this according to the law of Christ ... which means to love God and all neighbors...

But here comes the difficulty: an evil man can hardly be forced by compulsion to love God; for, indeed, the living of God depends on free will and on the love of man's heart, a love which originates in the word of God...

A good king could only by preaching the word of God persuade an evil people to love God; for otherwise, by forcing them he will not succeed. But if a king has to better a people by preaching ... he is not a king any more, he becomes a priest. As a king he could do naught but hang all evil men. For no king, not even the best one, could succeed in correcting an evil people except by the law of Christ. This law alone is capable of making sinful men better through their conscience. The king, having no power to force his people to obey this law, also has no authority to force their consciences, not to speak of the right to coerce their improvement through royal or civil laws; just as a fruit-tree cannot blossom in a winter season of cruel frosts, neither goodness can prosper through the laws of the Emperor...

Therefore, a Christian who takes account of his conscience must have no part in that office ... since his good intention cannot succeed with his exercise of its authority...

(The profession of government) is a heavy burden; not only does it weigh one down with its own burdens of sin, but even with the sins of the subjects; the sins which they committed by his orders or the sins which they committed (not by his orders) but which he could have prevented, they all fall upon his head. It becomes evident that only those who do not care about truth and who have no compassion can enjoy with good conscience offices with pagan lordship; authority becomes in their hand the law of injustice, enabling them to do what they want, not allowing their conscience to interfere with their willfulness. [The only precaution they take is that all iniquities and every violence are done according to the letter of the law.] To them can be rightly applied the parable of the trees found in the Jewish Law which says:

Once upon a time the trees set out to anoint a king over themselves; so they said to the olive tree, "Reign over us." But the olive tree said to them, "Do I lack my rich oil with which gods and men are honored, that I should go begging to the trees?" Then the trees said to the fig tree, "Do

138

you come and reign over us." But the fig tree said to them, "Do I lack my sweetness and good fruit that I should go begging to the trees? Then the trees said to the vine, "Do you come and reign over us." But the vine said to them, "Do I lack my wine, which cheers gods and men, that I should go begging to the trees? Finally the trees said to the thorn, "Do you come and reign over us." But the thorn said to the trees, "If in good faith you are anointing me as king over you, come and take shelter in my shade; but if not, fire shall burst forth from the thorn, and consume the cedars of Lebanon!"

CHAPTER 37

THE LAW OF MEN AND THE LAW OF CHRIST (CONTINUED)

First, the trees came to the olive tree asking it to reign over them; but the olive tree refused; it has substance suitable in men's food and useful in medicines. It signifies men abounding in divine grace who are filled with the Spirit and who are the medicine for the sorrows and sufferings of men. The fig tree has delicious fruit that contains both little seeds as well as honey; it signifies the loving brotherhood in which a multitude becomes one body of Christ. The vine contains satisfaction and joy; it signifies good conscience pertaining to communion at a divine feast, for only there conscience is a constant feast and the mind in safety. That is why all these tasty fruit trees refused to rule and to be exalted above other wild (fruit-less) trees lest they lose their fat substance, sweetness, and consolation.

Let us see what many useful things this parable can show us. [People who are partakers of the gifts of God will not forfeit these for the sake of temporal advantages, prestige, and authority, seeing that these 'advantages' entail violence and cruelty.] But the true word of God says, "The earth is the Lord's and its fullness, that is, its mountains, and valleys, and all regions." God is the only rightful ruler of this earth.

[And what title has the nobility to the land and people? It got it by tricks.] He who is not God's has no right to possess or to hold anything that belongs to God, unless he has taken possession of it illegally and by violence. Thus, contrary to the divine law, our fathers bought and established illegal claims for us ... and this is our natural heritage: poverty, shame, and death, and after that, hell. [Shame, trickery, falsehood, and cruelty – these are the true signs of our coats-of-arms. But God shall regard all these unlawful property holders as traitors of the kingdom of God.]

And if you who are heavy and round with fat object, saying, "Our fathers have bought these people and those manors for our inheritance," then, indeed, they made an evil business and an expensive bargain! For who has the right to buy people, to enslave them and to treat them with indignities as if they were cattle led to slaughter? You prefer dogs to people whom you cuss, despise, and beat, from whom you extort taxes and for whom you forge fetters ... while at the same time you will say to your dog, "Setter, come here and lie down on the pillow." Those people were God's before you bought them!

Who has the right to buy people? They were God's and ... after they were enslaved ... Christ Jesus bought this people to himself, not with silver or gold, but with his own precious blood and terrible suffering. He loves one human being more than all the riches of the earth together... The heavenly Lord redeems and buys (the people) for his inheritance. And the earthly lord buys them in order to increase his pleasures through their pain, to make a bridge out of their bent backs, to make himself a soft bed by their labor; and he puts on them all the burden of his groaning table (as rich men have), of his bright and soft garments and other physical pleasures. Look, you fat one, what a sodomitic life you have prepared for your people! What will you say on the Day of Judgment when the Lord will seat Himself on the judgment seat, and when all injustices committed against this people – yes, the very people who He Himself bought with His blood – will be arraigned against you? And He will say to you, "As you did it to one of the least of these my brethren, you did it to me. Go to hell!"

140

... And no high titles, no archives, no records, no documents with seals ... will save you from perdition.

CHAPTER 38

THE LAW OF MEN AND THE LAW OF CHRIST (CONCLUSION)

[Chelčický recapitulates his account of how the early Church remained faithful to Christ for the first three hundred and twenty years, how the Emperor and the Pope made an alliance, bartering their powers, and how the faith became corrupted with the defilement of the Church.]

But remember this, Christians who follow faith and arrange their life accordingly cannot in truth rule over each other in the manner of pagan rulership. A Christian lord cannot buy people and rule over them...

CHAPTER 39

THE EVILS OF THE CHURCH OF ROME – LUKE 3:14

[Here Chelčický begins a new section. In the preceding chapters he analyzed the evils of the temporal power. In the following chapters he will look closer to the evils of the Church of Rome.]

The things that we have said heretofore are a laughing matter and a blasphemy and a cause of anger ... to the great men of the Church of Rome...

The Church of Rome ... intoxicated as it is by poison, wants to lead wars, to squeeze blood out of men, and to render evil for evil; for all this it needs the strong secular power.

141

[It misinterprets the Scriptures in order to justify its warfare. The Church misinterprets even the answer that St. John gave to the soldiers who asked him, "What shall we do?" "Rob no one by violence or by false accusation, and be content with your wages." The next chapters will deal with the interpretation of this text.]

CHAPTER 40

INTERPRETATION OF LUKE 3:14

REFUTATION OF ST. AUGUSTINE'S

ARGUMENT ON PERMISSIBLE WARFARE

[The temporal power, bad as it is, could not of itself sharpen so many swords for the Christians.] But that 'great pillar' of the Church of Rome, who supports it strongly so that it may not fall, gave to the gospel a spirit of a sharp sword when he said, "If Christian discipline were to disparage war completely, this should be found in the gospel ordering us to put down arms and give up soldiering; however, it is satisfied with the admonition not to exact too much and to be content with wages. It does not attack the calling of the soldier." This 'great pillar' has thus extracted blood instead of milk out of the gospel. If our faith were founded on such acts of bloodiness (*sic*) – and how much blood there was spilled by the soldiers because of this teaching – then it would be correct. But our faith obliges us to bind wounds, not to make blood run...

And he says about the Christian discipline that when the soldiers came to John to be baptized saying, "And we, what must we do?" John should he have given them another answer: "Throw your weapons away, give up war service, wound and kill no one." According to these arguments, it would seem necessary for the Roman Church to fight, to shed human blood, and to gain peace by the sword... For this reason there is a need of soldiers who would go to war for the Holy Church and for Country. According to this (view) warfare among Christians is a good thing and founded on

Scriptures… Therefore, when that 'pillar' was standing in Rome holding and supporting the Church and providing her with a scripturally sanctioned warfare, some came forth objecting on the basis of Christian discipline; but he accused them of being heretics and their discipline but a foul error. [Now it is natural that the Church, leaning against the secular power, does everything she can to bolster up that 'pillar', lest it fall down with its strange teaching.]

Now of course, we have to obey the Scripture … but not everything in the Scripture is divine… Some portions do not lead us to follow Christ for (they) were written by some only as an (historical) record, and they were never (intended) to have any power. So, for example, when our Lord Jesus cured the lepers he told them to go to show themselves to the priests and to offer gifts in accordance with the Law of Moses. Therefore, even though this was recorded in the Scripture, later on no apostle ever sent cured lepers to the Jewish priests, nor was any Christian obligated to give thank-offerings in accordance with the Law of Moses. This was written as an (historic) act of the power of Jesus and of a custom of the priests of the Old Testament, but not for an imitation by coming generations of Christians.

The story of John and his soldiers must be understood in a similar manner. He did certain things and spoke in a certain way, which Lord Jesus neither did nor spoke… And we understand that John was sent before Lord Jesus to prepare his way, that is, to move the people to repentance and to an expectation of Lord Jesus, saying that he who will come after him will be greater… Therefore John, who preceded our Lord Jesus in time, was still under the Law of Moses, which he was bound to observe in all his acts and words – excepting baptism and bearing witness to Jesus; this was outside the Law… But John could not have changed the laws (concerning) the (established) order of things.

CHAPTER 41

REFUTATION OF AUGUSTINE'S ARGUMENT

(CONCLUSION)

The soldiers who came to John with their question were not of the Christian faith. And John, seeing they were people accustomed to serve commanders and rulers, gave them an answer that was in agreement with the Law of Moses: "Rob no one by violence and be content with your wages." For those sins come easiest to those who rely on the power of compulsion... John did not dissuade them from soldiering, since the Jews were allowed to perform military service and to conduct defensive wars against enemies... He only tried to restrain them from evils they might easily succumb to in their profession...

John could not have said, "Leave soldiering and follow me." But Lord Jesus had the authority to say to the ruler, "Sell all that you possess, give it to the poor, and follow me." He had even power to change his claim to nobility, to ask him to leave his wife and to follow Jesus. He did not order him to defend the church by the sword lest she be blown down by a contrary wind...

[This story about John and the soldiers] was not written for the purpose of showing Christians that ... they need military service for the defense of faith or of faithful people. [It only asks everyone to be faithful to his profession, to his faith.] And the Christians must be faithful to the teaching of their Jesus ... who taught them to turn the other cheek if anyone struck them on the right cheek, not to return evil for evil, and to love their enemies.

What will the knights with their sword do about this? That 'pillar' who supports the Church in her bloody business is afraid lest Christian discipline should hasten condemning war, and (in doing so) he justifies war in the Christian religion on Jewish kings and their law, and even on pagan kings. The Church teaches the Christian kings to defend her by war against external enemies and by exterminating heretics (who are the

144

domestic enemies) … by virtue of the example of Jewish kings…

CHAPTER 42

INTERPRETATION OF ROMANS 13:1-2

Now we shall struggle with the words of Saint Paul who says, "Let every person be subject to the governing authorities. For there is no authority except from God, and those that exist have been instituted by God."

The ruling princes of the Christian secular power find in these words their crowning witness, concluding that this text was given by Saint Paul to the Christians of Rome and that all princes are thereby established in their authority. And the doctors desire that this be accepted as faith by all Christians. As it was said to me by a doctor of the Prague University, namely, that I should believe it this way; that I am a heretic if I do not believe it.

Now we must be very careful to understand the words of Saint Paul, to see what he meant. He wrote to a small group of Christians in Rome, which was a pagan city ruled by pagan kings… Paul makes a great distinction: he asks the Christians to be humbly subjected to pagan rulers in all temporal matters. But it is quite another matter to ask them to elevate a ruler from their own Christian ranks and to defend their rights by force. It is one thing to teach Christians to be subject to foreign powers in reasonable matters, and it is another thing to rule and to appoint princes contrary to other princes.

[The princes are committing a great sin if they twist the teaching of Jesus and his apostles in order to perpetuate pagan evils,] to persecute the Christians for faith, to keep them in prison for faith, and to execute them in the name of faith. [Some of the executed men were saints, and often the princes – executioners – were the worst criminals.]

It was the same cruel pagan authority, filled with many stings, hiding true Christian religion behind a mock-faith, that caused suffering and martyrdom to the real faithful ones, to the faithful Hus and Jerome; the King of Hungary thus caused, by his own hands, that they should attain heavenly glory.

CHAPTER 43

INTERPRETATION OF ROMANS 13:1-2 (CONTINUED)

So it happened that the authority in Rome of which Paul was speaking was pagan. And he exhorted the Christians to be patiently obedient to that authority (even though) it persecuted them for their faith... And those who have written chronicles of those days and of the Christian martyrdoms ... say there were thirteen emperors in Rome, from the time of Paul to the days of Constantine, and every one of them was a pagan, murdering faithful Christians for their faith; ... they murdered Saint Peter, and thirty-five bishops after him, until the days of Sylvester, and all for faith... This lasted three hundred and twenty years...

[Therefore it is wrong to construe from Paul's words that all authority is sanctioned by the Christian faith. Such assertions can be made only by priests who are intoxicated by the poison of power. Through power, they have converted faith into a lucrative business.] And they pushed out the poor and humble Jesus; he is their ruler no more.

CHAPTER 44

INTERPRETATION OF ROMANS 13:1-2 (CONTINUED)

When Saint Paul said, "Let every soul be subject to higher powers," he was reminding the congregation of the faithful Christians in Rome ... to obey the pagan authority of Caesar. He had in mind ... their condition and righteousness... He wanted them to avoid all conflict with the pagans,

146

and to excel in Christian virtues, repaying no one evil for evil, but taking thought for what is noble in the sight of all. And, since it is noble in the sight of the pagans to pay taxes, let the Christians do likewise. Such subordination comes from humility.

These things befit the servants of God; they should be subject in humility … not only to good but even bad authorities.

[This subjection must be passive, however, and not of the character of an active participation.]

CHAPTER 45

INTERPRETATION OF ROMANS 13:1-2 (CONTINUED)

The second reason for Paul's words is this: [Everything is to be done orderly and peacefully. The authorities sometimes have the same aim. And the Christians should help them in this, all the more considering that this is what God requires of them. Men of faith do good without waiting to be compelled to it by laws. Also, there are many who, being liberated through the grace of God from the burden of the old law, interpret this freedom as unchecked liberty, giving them a free hand to rebel against their overlords.]

This thought often moves, even today, good and bad people who, greatly desiring freedom, think of how to humiliate and unseat their lords so that these will not override them. Therefore, Saint Peter, seeing this, calls this freedom a pretext for evil, which wrongly obstructs true freedom Desiring the freedom of Christ much too physically, they object to being subjected to higher powers who, however, enslave them as guilty, depriving them even of that little freedom of conscience and body they had.

[That is why Paul urges the Christians to be submissive toward their pagan overlords:]

Let every person be subject to the governing authorities; for there is no authority except from God; and those that exist have been instituted by God.

There is no authority except from God. That is, there is no other power, good or bad, pagan or heretic, which is a true authority, according to the Scripture. [However, God uses these 'evil' authorities to chastise a rebellious people.]

As it is happening among us in these days, for almost fifteen years a raging mad authority is destroying everything, caring naught about a just administration of villages, but rather being anxious to destroy, to prostrate, to scorch, to murder, to rob, to imprison, and to devastate everything like a plague of locusts. God has allowed this evil to happen because He wanted to pour out His anger on the sinful people who do not honor Him but, on the contrary, are dishonoring Him by hypocrisy. This power could not have arisen, had He not desired it; for, as the prophet says, "if there be disaster in the city, has not the Lord caused it?"

[What Paul actually means is this: let the Christians be subject to temporal authorities in externals, but let them remember that the true authority is only the authority of God. Only under that authority can they fully live the Beatitudes. And the Scripture says about those powers that contradict the authority of God that] the mighty will be mightily tested.

[In Paul's days there were no Christian authorities but only pagan authorities. And these authorities were sanctioned by the God of the Old Testament.]

Were it not so, Paul could not have exhorted the faithful Christians of Rome to obey Emperor Nero the pagan, saying, "There is no authority except from God." [But this authority of the pagans cannot make them better men. It is only by accepting the faith in Jesus Christ that they are given the power to become sons of God, and to be better than the pagans. Then the pagan power becomes irrelevant.] But in reality we do not see that the Christians excel over pagans with their goodness; rather, they excel the pagans in iniquities. Outwardly, with their lips, they confess

Jesus Christ, but inwardly they hate faith… Instead of faith they have thin water in which they dip the name of Jesus… They get away from him as if he were a debt they cannot pay. And, since they are in no wise better than the pagans, they cannot be saved by their authority – even though it is sanctioned by God – unless they seek salvation in Christ's faith, as the Scripture says,False is the king, and the king cannot be saved by the power of his own authority.

It says that the king is false, even though authority has been divinely bestowed upon him; … he shall not be saved on account of his injustice.

CHAPTER 46

INTERPRETATION OF ROMANS 13:1-2 (CONTINUED)

[The nominal Christians pervert the words of Paul, giving them a meaning to serve their own interests. Therefore, it is very important for those who want to be true Christians to see the true meaning of those words.]

For the word of God concerns sometimes (a) the true heavenly and spiritual authorities, and (b) the true spiritual authorities that are a little lower than the heavenly: the creaturely … authorities … I do not intend nor am I able to expound on the spiritual and heavenly authorities that are of God; I shall be concerned only about the human institutions that should be perfect in God's spiritual order as well as in the lower earthly orders. The latter, which God has established since the beginning of time, has been lost. Having lost that order they dwell now in great disorder. But even though they live in this disorder, they still need some form of order that could – if not improve them – at least keep them in their corporeal life.

[God established this order by giving man a twofold nature, one perishable, and the other imperishable. One generation dies, but the other generation is born, having its foundation in the union of father and

149

mother. Mankind respects the family institution that maintains stability and order, propriety as well as property.]

But because these generations are born in sin, filled with iniquities, the devils rule over them. Therefore, Saint Paul says about them that they are princes of the power of the air, who are at work in the sons of disobedience that is, in the princes of darkness and in the rulers of the world. Through their hatred and iniquity, death was ushered into the whole orbit of the earth

[God gave to the temporal authorities the right to rule over regions so that they might control the people and settle all their differences peacefully. Authority maintains order by compulsion. It must be a wise authority if it is to rule over unwise men.] King Ahasverus ... knew of this rule ... and therefore he said,Having become a ruler of many nations, and come to have dominion over the whole world, I desire, not because I am elated by the presumption of power but behaving always with mildness and moderation, to insure that my subjects shall live in unbroken tranquility, and in order to make my kingdom peaceable and to reestablish the peace which all men desire

CHAPTER 47

INTERPRETATION OF ROMANS 13:1-2 (CONTINUED)

[It is the responsibility of the pagan rulers to preserve peace. But the devil always seeks how to prevent or pervert this order.] He led the first two human brothers to do evil and to murder because of hatred He does this in every generation, (and every generation has its own Cains). The secular sovereignty ... is like a fence, supposed to preserve the lost sheep for a later time of salvation... But when mankind arouses the anger of God ... no fence can resist His wrath. Then kings make wars and inflict all kinds of sufferings... That is why Samuel said to the Jewish people,See the king whom you have chosen; if you persist in wrongdoing, both you and your king shall be swept away

For all men and their kings are foolish The Master Adversary says that royal sovereignty and civil authority … began with Cain's lust for power when he built the first city According to the Chronicle of Josephus this foundation of the city was the cause of increasing gathering of possessions and of violent robberies; Cain fortified the city because he feared them whom he had in any way despoiled. Therefore, the beginning of power and sovereignty is to be found in human cupidity and violence. Wherefore Solomon says to the kings,

"Listen, O Kings, and take warning, O Judges of the earth. Incline your ears, you who boast of ruling over multitudes of nations, and who enjoy being the first For He will come upon you terribly and swiftly, for a stern judgment overtakes those in high places

CHAPTER 48

INTERPRETATION OF ROMANS 13:1-2 (CONTINUED)

[Even the worst ruler must appeal to his people by virtue of his opposition to evil powers. He must speak in terms of justice done even to the least subject of his realm. He is, unwittingly, comparing his rule to that perfect rule of God. In doing this he acknowledges God's priority.]

David and other kings … who had the knowledge of God … could rule over the people according to the law of God, and even use compulsion… But the Jewish law was a material, physical law, and therefore they were allowed to use physical compulsion with regard to the disobedient.

CHAPTER 49

INTERPRETATION OF ROMANS 13:1-2 (CONTINUED)

[The kings according to the old dispensation ruled the people by law. They did not punish robbery by execution but by restitution The rulers of today, however, even though they call themselves Christian, abide by neither the new nor the old law; they kill the robber.] And it is said in the New Testament, Let the thief no longer steal, but rather let him labor, doing honest work with his hands, so that he may be able to give to those in need

[The Christian kings do not heed these principles.] There are some who do not have even as much sense as to be able to settle a small dispute between two peasants. (All they know is to hang and to torture.) The divine element is much smaller in the rule of Christian kings than it was in the rule of pagan and Jewish kings. Therefore, because both divine institutions, marriage and temporal rule, were unable to achieve perfection, God sent His Son, the Savior of the world, in order that we might live through him And he rules the world with greater perfection by means of truth than all the kings of the earth by means of compulsion.

CHAPTER 50

INTERPRETATION OF ROMANS 13:1-2 (CONTINUED)

[Following Christ's appearance on earth, man is bound to love God and His new order with all his heart, mind, and soul, and to submit voluntarily to His discipline in order to become a real man of God. Man's earthly life passes quickly away but the eternal life abides forever.]

Whatever divine sanction there is in human establishments, it applies to the earthly, temporal life. The new law, introduced by the Son of God, applies to the earthly things very little, and sometimes not at all. Its applications to earthly things are:

152

If you have food and clothing, with these you shall be content; and i anyone would sue you and take your clothing, let it rest at that. Give him your cloak as well

And if they take your goods by violence, rejoice, believing that they are not lost, for in heaven you will find worthier goods than the tempora (ones you lost).

Christ's new order leaves man with the hope in God so that, throwing al his cares to God, he would not sin for temporal goods, believing that to take care of one's neighbor is much more important.

[Christ's dominion presents a remedy for soul and body, for man and society, and is incomparably better than any human institution and law.]

CHAPTER 51

INTERPRETATION OF ROMANS 13:1-2 (CONTINUED)

And this is what Paul had in mind when he said, "He who resists the authority resists what God has appointed, and those who resist will incur judgment

[In other words, if the authority requires things contrary to the will of God, it is not "appointed by God" but incited by pride. Any exercise of authority contrary to the will of God is untrue, sinful, and not binding to the Christian. And "those who resist will incur the judgment" of the men in authority. Therefore, even though a Christian may consider sovereignty an unnecessary and harmful evil, he should not resist it with hatred curses, and base action. If he did, he would act contrary to the will of God whose command is to love.]

153

CHAPTER 52

INTERPRETATION OF ROMANS 13:1-2 (CONTINUED)

[It may well be that there is a government actually endeavoring to insure justice toward all and peace among the factions. It is, however, much more natural for a state to be oppressive.] The greatest cause for which so many resist the state authority is found in the imposition of heavy burdens of taxation, compulsory services, required field work, and many other injustices. The subjects are sinful through their impatience, seeking revenge against those who are in authority over them, and they curse them; thus the lords sin in committing injustices, and the subjects sin in feeling revengeful towards their lords. [As a Christian, bear patiently all injustices, and your patience will be added to your credit in the world to come.] If you do not want to go to the forest, singing even during a storm, of your own accord, you will be compelled to go there weeping, and they shall beat you over your head. Thus, you resist in vain the current of the river; you may cross it with humility, but you cannot slow it down with your grumbling.

CHAPTER 53

INTERPRETATION OF ROMANS 13:1-2 (CONTINUED)

Now many, including ourselves, resist the governing authorities for another reason, supposing that this resistance is justified and condoned by faith... The priesthood has been invested with power and riches by the Emperor, and it has allied itself with his authority so that it might cover up its evil and hypocritical life. Therefore, it praises this authority for its own advantage, and even includes it in its structure of faith as an integral part.

Therefore we repeat that the secular governing authority is compulsory, and therefore not in the position to be of very much help to faith. [It is spiritually weak, appeasing consciences by giving out occasional crumbs of goodness; this enables it to maintain a semblance of order, at least for

154

the time being. This is, in effect, what the secular authorities say to the Church:] "Priests, do not eat your bread for nothing! Drive your flock to the lords so that they may watch over it with their swords and nasty goats!" [And we say to the state:] "And you, sons of the scepter, sit render account and repent for cheating the people of their souls and possessions!"

CHAPTER 54

INTERPRETATION OF ROMANS 13:1-2 (CONTINUED)

[When the authorities commit such perversions and sins, the Christian is not obligated to obey them, and this because of the following Biblical examples:]

- ▶ The three young men did not resist the royal authority of King Nebuchadnezzar sinfully; on the contrary, they were saved by God in the trial of the fiery furnace.
- ▶ Mordecai did not sin by refusing to do obeisance to Hasan. He obeyed God rather than men
- ▶ The Jews who resisted the order of King Antiochus Epiphanes to bow down before Greek gods and who were murdered for their obstinacy, did not sin

CHAPTER 55

INTERPRETATION OF ROMANS 13:1-2 (CONCLUSION)

Also, some of the Doctors of the Church taught the people saying, "Let the humble be admonished that they be obedient not more than is proper, that they be not compelled to honor compulsory sins; for there will be some who will desire the people to be submissive more than is proper; let it be known that evil must never be exercised by way of obedience."

[Obey in good things; disobey in evil things.] Even if he who is above all other apostles should preach something contrary to the will of God, he should not be obeyed:

Even if we, or an angel from heaven, should preach to you a gospel contrary to that which we preached to you, let him be accursed

[That means, if secular authority exercises its power in accordance with the sovereignty of God, it is not contrary to His will. If it exercises power in a direction contrary to His supreme authority, it sins. And to obey such sinful governing authorities means to be partakers of their sin.]

And to obey the princes or the prelates in these compulsory sinful acts is tantamount to honoring their sins and thus also the devil. If we remembered the Church Doctors who said that the subjects should not obey their authorities in matters forbidden by God, with whom could they go to war? For they run to war doing to their neighbors that which God has forbidden and which would not be tolerated at home. The commandment of God says, "So whatever you wish that men would do to you, do so to them. But he who goes to war does evil to them of whom he would wish that they do good to him; and what he would be loath doing at home, that he gladly does obeying the orders of his lords...

If all the Christian people should obey the commandments of God, how many of them would be imprisoned, and what great rivers of blood would flow from the martyrs of the paganized authorities! For (faithful Christians) would refuse to storm the walls, to run like cattle, to destroy, to murder, and to rob; instead, obeying their faith, they would rather perish under the sword than to do these things so revolting to the law of God. But here, this foolish cattle, dipped in holy water, has turned its back to God and His law, gladly doing everything evil, seduced as it is by the Church of Rome, and drunken by the wine of the great harlot with whom the kings of the earth have committed fornication, bathing the world in blood and iniquities

CHAPTER 56

INTERPRETATION OF ROMANS 13:3-4

Saint Paul goes on to say:

For rulers are not a terror to good conduct, but to bad. Would you have no fear of him who is in authority? Then do what is good, and you will receive his approval, for he is God's servant for your good

Here we are always caught between the fences, as it were, when we look to the interpretations of the Church of Rome (derived from the Emperor) and it is difficult to get to the true intention of Saint Paul's meaning. [The Church applies these words to any authority and any prince. This interpretation caused the enslavement of the people. But Paul always spoke of the rulers who lived before the time of Jesus Christ, who were not Christian, and when as yet nobody ever heard of the Christians. The Church gives her interpretation in order to please the rulers and thus to induce them to join her. But in Paul's days the pagan rulers persecuted the Christians. Having those cruel princes in mind, Paul says to the Christians: "Obey your authorities, do good, and do not antagonize the authorities against yourselves."]

And concerning the sentence, "rulers are not a terror to good conduct but to bad," we must remember that the rulers were pagans. How then could they be able to distinguish between good and bad deeds? [The Roman rulers and princes knew legal goodness only. That is, they were concerned with checking crass injustices, violence, theft, disputes, murders, robber bands, bandits, and adulteries. They checked these evils by their authority of compulsion. If they did not do so, their kingdom would perish.]

For even among pagans peacefulness is a great virtue... The gospel praises the saintly people Zechariah and Elisabeth that they were both righteous before God, walking blamelessly in all the commandments and ordinances of the Lord They lived virtuously, for no one sued them and they in turn did not dispute with anyone. Therefore, nobody could bring complaint against them, unless it was done by false witness and jealousy.

157

That is what Saint Paul means when he says, "the rulers are not a terror to good conduct, but to bad."

CHAPTER 57

INTERPRETATION OF ROMANS 13:3-4 (CONTINUED)

[The justice and righteousness according to Christ is an altogether different matter. The pagans do not understand it and, therefore, persecute its adherents.] Paul could not have said, "Do good, and you shall be praised for it." Both Christ and his apostles did good, yet they did not ingratiate themselves to the authorities. Instead, they were put to death because of their good works. Saint Paul did nothing but good, professing in Rome the name of Christ; he did not ingratiate himself to Nero nor did he win his praises, but on the contrary lost his life by his order. [Do good, says Paul, and you shall receive the approval not of the authorities but of God. The apostle well makes a distinction between the justice of faith and that of the rulers when he says,]

Among the mature we do impart wisdom, although it is not a wisdom of this age or of the rulers of this age, who are doomed to pass away. But we impart a secret and hidden wisdom of God, which God decreed before the ages for our glorification. None of the rulers of this age understood this; for if they had, they would not have crucified the Lord of glory

[They crucified him even though he brought people back to life. They hated his message and the Christians of Rome had to separate on that account from the pagan rulers. This gave them freedom to resist authorities by virtue of the same principle that made the Jews of the old days resist the compulsion of Nebuchadnezzar, Ahasuerus, and Antiochus They were morally obligated to obey the authority of God, even though that meant their death at the hands of the secular authority.]

CHAPTER 58

INTERPRETATION OF ROMANS 13:3-4 (CONTINUED)

[Faith in Jesus Christ was the real cause of persecutions of the Christian community in Rome. They were a small minority in the midst of a pagan majority.] However, God ruled over the Christians, the pagans, and their mighty emperors. For the pagans could not pluck even a hair from the heads of the faithful without His will Therefore, if they were killed, it was in accordance with His will; He wanted to test His servants and to magnify their glory through their martyrdom; He did not tempt them beyond their strength, but provided, along with the temptation, also a way of escape, that they might be able to endure it [In this way the pagans were an instrument of the faith of Christ hidden in the hands of God. But the true faith is always unknown and hidden to the rulers and pagans as well as the unfaithful Christians.] The knowledge and the wisdom of the faith of Christ is hidden from those who seek God in a painted wall, and no one can discover this hidden secret unless it is given from above, by God. Being hidden and secret it is contrary to the world and the world despises it. A world faithfully praying to painted walls cannot know God. This world, which seeks God on the surface, is like a goat gnawing the outer bark of a willow; the power and aliveness of faith is hidden from it.

Therefore, speaking of faith, it is wrong to say, "Do what is good, and you will be praised for it, unless the life of faith had preserved the Christians. They may have received praise from other (faithful), but none from Emperor Nero.

CHAPTER 59

INTERPRETATION OF ROMANS 13:3-4 (CONTINUED)

To this Paul adds, "The servant of God is for your good." On this word hangs all the assurance of the Church, and the Church Doctors deduce from it all ecclesiastical authority to the great comfort of the powerful priesthood. They say that with these words St. Paul confirmed the position of Christ's servant with the sword, namely, the supreme lord the Emperor, for the benefit and protection of the great and holy mother – the Church of Rome – and of all the sons born of her, in order that she and her sons might not suffer the untowardness of the cross, that she be not bothered by contrary winds, that he might bear her temptations with his sword, to enable her to recite her matins unmolested, and to sing and direct her litanies and praises to God.

Therefore, let no one rebuke the servant of God and of the sword, for the servant of God is a very great blessing to the Church. The sword of the servant of God is the peace of the Church. Let no one blame the hosts of knights for they exist for the good of the Church; let no one criticize the burgomasters, the councilors, the bailiffs, the executioners, the town-halls, the jails, the bilboes, or the racks, for all these are the instruments of the servant of God. With them he does the will of God and a service to the Church, the power of governing and of executing is the foundation of the wealth and self-sufficiency of the Church.

The apostles of the original Church of Christ were all bearing the weapons of executive and punitive authority on their necks, on their sides, and on their bodies, they were bathed in blood and condemned to death by the instruments of the executioner for the name of Christ; and now these same instruments are for the protection of the Church, used for the shedding of the blood of those who resist the Church and who criticize her avariciousness and simony through the truth of the gospel of Christ!

CHAPTER 60

INTERPRETATION OF ROMANS 13:3-4 (CONTINUED)

[Let us go to the Scripture to see what is meant by the expression "servant of God." It cannot be given the sole meaning that the Church of Rome attaches to it. In the Scripture we find the words:]

You established the earth and it stood fast. By your ordinances they stand today, for all things are your servants

All things serve God which do His will... God wills it that birds should exist until the end of the world; and so a bird builds a nest, lays eggs and brings up little birds; in doing this it fulfills the will of God, and the bird is a "servant of God." It is God's will that men multiply by birth; therefore, when a woman bears the children of men, she does the will of God and is His servant... Good men and bad men do the will of God, some better, some worse... But how could that pagan, the Emperor of Rome, the unfaithful idolater, the murderer and persecutor of the apostles and many faithful Christians, be called a servant of God? [They who live by faith are the true servants of God. He is the sovereign of the world, ruling over peoples and kings.] The Scripture says:

Listen, therefore, kings, and understand. Pay attention, rulers of the people, who boast of multitudes of nations, for your dominion was given you from the Lord, and your sovereignty from the Most High. He will examine your works and inquire into your plans, for though you are servants of his kingdom, you have not judged rightly or kept the Law or followed the will of God

Many a king does not know the King of Heaven, but he still is like a plough in the hands of the ploughman; the plough does not know what the ploughman intends. [The people of the earth are evil and would devour each other, did not the kings maintain some sort of order.]

God uses (the rulers) as a plaster on an abscess, so that the evils will not spread. If this medicine does not help, He sends other kings in their stead, as He had done with the stiff-necked Jews...

161

CHAPTER 61

INTERPRETATION OF ROMANS 13:3-4 (CONTINUED)

[With all their evils, are kings servants of God? The Bible gives the answer:] Nebuchadnezzar, the King of Babylon, was a great king and a very evil tyrant. And yet, God ordered all the earth to submit to the power of the King of Babylon... Therefore, when the Jews hardened and refused to obey the will of God, He ordered the prophet Jeremiah to say to the Jews:

Because you have not listened to my words, behold, I am sending for a family from the north, and will bring them against this land and its inhabitants, and against all these nations round about; and I will utterly destroy them, and will make them a horror, a scorn, and an everlasting reproach; and I will banish from them the sound of mirth and the sound of gladness

Nebuchadnezzar was a servant of God in that he ... became an instrument of His wrath. [That is why Paul calls the evil and cruel kings "servants of God." But this does not mean that the priests of the Church should praise these Caesars and emulate their deeds and techniques, incorporating them as an article of faith into a system for the defense of the Church.]

CHAPTER 62

INTERPRETATION OF ROMANS 13:3-4 (CONTINUED)

[However, the arguments of the Church and of her wise doctors in defense of authority are not Christian.]

Therefore, no Christian should deviate from the path of faith in order to follow the Emperor and his sword, for indeed, the way of Christ has not been repealed just because the Emperor is "Christian." In the beginning, the Christians were obligated to follow Christ in patience and humility,

162

and they were expected to persevere in this even under the Emperors. If they have rejected patience for the purpose of defending the Emperor, they have been seduced from faith by the Emperor; they no longer are of the faith of Christ but of the faith of the Emperor. He introduced the religion of the sword to the Christians. These were formerly beaten for the sake of Christ and were rewarded by him; now they stand guard with a sword, and expect to be rewarded by the Emperor. Where Caesar is, there they are too. Man shall be rewarded fittingly in accordance with what he believes.

CHAPTER 63

INTERPRETATION OF ROMANS 13:3-4 (CONTINUED)

[We cannot be true servants of God unless we follow the precepts of Christ. Secular authority is too much confused with evil and violence. Christ said,]

If anyone serves me, he must follow me; and where I am, there shall my servant be also; if anyone serves me, the Father will honor him

Therefore, to serve God according to Christ's faith means to follow his example in patience, in humility, in poverty, and in saving work. It is an extraordinary thing that the world cannot recognize this service; neither can an evil man recognize it, but only he whom He chooses; for it depends on the true love of God – a love which the world has not, knows not, and cannot comprehend, since it is filled with evil graces contrary to the Divine love. A dirty barrel ... cannot be a fitting container for new wine; similarly, the service of God cannot be confused with the ways of this world... [Serve God, or serve Nero and the pope – you cannot serve both.]

CHAPTER 64

INTERPRETATION OF ROMANS 13:3-4 (CONTINUED)

Says Saint Paul about the servants:

If you do wrong, be afraid, for he does not bear the sword in vain; he is the servant of God to execute his wrath on the wrong-doer

[The pagan ruler, says Paul, is the rod of God's anger, and therefore His servant.] It would be little virtue, akin to pagan virtue, if the Christians were doing good only because of fearing the sword. Before this (passage) Paul wrote them about fear saying,

For you did not receive the spirit of slavery to fall back into fear, but you have received the spirit of sonship. When we cry, "Abba, Father!" it is the Spirit himself bearing witness with our spirit that we are children of God, and if children, then heirs, heirs of God and fellow heirs with Christ, provided we suffer with him in order that also we may be glorified with him.

He who does good because of the fear of the sword may save his physical life, (from the threat of the sword). Therefore, I have said that Saint Paul, considering the inclination of this people to do good works by the grace of God, spoke about the sword on account of an especial carefulness and goodwill toward the lords to whom they were subordinated. But had this people been living in the Promised Land, like the sons of Israel in their days of freedom, when they had no secular lord with authority over them, Saint Paul would never have written that they ought to do good and to eschew evil in the fear of the sword. For they had too good a rule given them by the apostles, and had no need to be prodded to goodness by the authority of the sword... [Paul certainly did not act contrary to the feelings of Samuel who regretted that the Jews preferred a king to freedom under God. He simply urged them to show Christian submission to their rulers, and to suffer their injustice with Christ-like patience.] The non-Christians, fearing the retribution of the sword, do not transgress the laws of their king. [In this way the kings are serving God] for they preserve

164

from annihilation the fallen generation [keeping it for God's own time.] God alone knows why he wants to have this generation saved and maintained by paganism.

CHAPTER 65

INTERPRETATION OF ROMANS 13:3-4 (CONTINUED)

[The pagans do good only because they are driven by fear of punishment.] That is why Saint Paul warns the Christians: "Be good and beware lest you fall into the hands of the pagans." No great harm is done when pagans sue pagans; they know no better way… [But when Christians commit some wrong and are tried in pagan courts, they appeal to pagan authority and confess that their faith is impotent to solve disputes. They are, in fact, renouncing the authority of Christ and expect a verdict from the authority of the sword; and this is to be avoided.]

CHAPTER 66

INTERPRETATION OF ROMANS 13:3-4 (CONTINUED)

Our own authorities are pagan… Our secularized priesthood loves authority, as it guarantees an easy life of comfort. [And, since the Church has allied itself with the secular authority, the injunction that St. Paul made to the faithful in Rome is not valid any more. For the Church herself has become a secular power. She defends herself in the same way as any state does.] The admonition, "do good if you do not want to fear the authority," has become pointless because … both the state and church authority have lost the moral right to punish evil … when they themselves are steeped in all evils… All they care about … is that (the Christians) attend masses, vigils, and other formal ceremonies. The Church authority stakes the salvation of all on masses … and eternal prayers; she

165

intermittently sings psalms for the dead; in the end she always sings them out of hell... Now this authority has nothing left with which to threaten, because she can redeem the dead souls from hell by her ceremonious acts.

CHAPTER 67

INTERPRETATION OF ROMANS 13:3-4 (CONCLUSION)

[The Church has completely lost her moral right of judgment. She has become a fortress of authority and her strong ammunition is provided by her learned Doctors and Fathers who – with the cunning use of Biblical texts – sanction her revenges, wars, and murders.] As if we could not see that she does not follow the law when she busies her self with reprisals and wars; whenever she has some hosts available she fights and murders.

CHAPTER 68

REFUTATION OF THE ARGUMENTS OF AEGIDIUS

CARLERII PRESENTED AT THE COUNCIL OF BASIL

Now let us look at the arguments defending the power of the Church, as they were presented in the dispute between Master Aegidius and Nicholas, the Bishop of Písek, at Basel, concerning the article about the destruction of sins. Master Aegidius gave many reasons based on Church Doctors, and these were the official replies of the Council to Bishop Nicholas. I shall recount some of these (discussions) in order to make better known some of those happenings that were woven so long ago; but not through my will, says the Lord.

Among many arguments, Master Aegidius says that the civil law can punish certain things legally by death and that this does not contradict the law of the gospel. The Explanation says concerning the words "you shall not kill" that the judge does not kill the innocent, but that it is the law that does it... And God can kill since He is the giver of life and death: "It is I who slay, and bring to life" Therefore the kings whom God has authorized to rule can kill in the exercise of their justice. It is also said to the Romans that those who do such things deserve to die. And about the judges he says that they do not wear the sword in vain, but serve God. The judge is justified to condemn to death in accordance with the Scripture that says, "as for these enemies of mine, who did not want me to reign over them, bring them here and slay them before me!" Then he mentions also Cyprian who, referring to the place in the Old Testament where God says to the tribe,If someone entices you in your cities saying, "let us go and serve alien gods," show him no mercy but be sure to kill him; and you kill him first, and then they shall kill those who are in the city.

He says this in explanation of another text, "remembering the commandment, Matathias slaughtered those who offered sacrifices to the idols." And since these things were commanded before the arrival of Christ, they are all the more valid after his appearance...

CHAPTER 69

THE ARGUMENTS OF AEGIDIUS CARLERII

(CONTINUED)

Saint Augustine, speaking about the City of God, was standing on a bloody ground when he said, "If someone is killed justly, he is killed by the law and not by the lawyer." And Saint Jerome says, "It is not cruelty but kindliness to punish the sins for God." And by punishment he means death, as is evident by his examples of Phinehas and his justice, the justice of Elijah, the justice of Simon of Canaan who sent fiery serpents on the magicians, the justice of Peter in punishing Ananias and Sapphira, the justice of Paul who humbled Elymas the magician, and he adds, "If your own brother, or friend, or wife should dare to defile truth, let your hand fall upon them and shed their blood." So much for Jerome. The old saints have certainly gathered enough food for the sword so that it would not starve! [All these arguments are false, and mean only to confuse the issues and to justify violence.]

CHAPTER 70

THE ARGUMENTS OF AEGIDIUS CARLERII

(CONTINUED)

St. Gregory says, "the commandment 'you shall not kill' forbids anyone to kill a man, but not to hand over to death a man condemned by the law." For he who exercises public authority and punishes the evil-doers by virtue of the law is not a transgressor of the commandment "you shall not kill." And Saint Augustine, speaking of the City of God, says:

When a soldier kills a man while serving under the state authority, he is not guilty of murder. On the contrary, if he refuses to obey the order to kill, he is guilty of insubordination.

He wallows in blood saying this. So, the soldier is obeying the law when he mercilessly murders people, but is a transgressor of the law if he should show mercy! This is what he says, he who is supposedly filled of the Holy Spirit! And again he says, that the House of David could not have had peace, had it not extinguished Absalom...

Master Aegidius used these as well as many other arguments in order to justify the right to spill blood by the secular authority. He quoted the Church Fathers, some of whom I have mentioned here, to show how much Christendom has been stained by blood through these learned Doctors... With their interpretations they are making God as having two mouths, with one saying "you shall not kill," and with the other, "you shall kill."

168

Who, then, can tell what God wants, when there are two ways, contrary to each other? (In doing this) men turn away from God.

CHAPTER 71

THE ARGUMENTS OF AEGIDIUS CARLERII

(CONTINUED)

[The Church defends warfare and violence with the reasonings of famous men, saintly men, and men full of the Holy Spirit.] They sanctioned with the Holy Spirit the spilling of blood committed by the Church... Yes, the Holy Spirit has gone into blood-letting for the peace of the holy mother Church.

Therefore, in order that their justifications might stand honorably and firmly among the Christians, they cunningly based their law on the words of Saint Paul who, condemning sins, said:

Though they know God's decree that those who do such things deserve to die, they do not only do them but also approve those who practice them.

The doctors interpret the words, "deserve to die," as sanctioning civil courts and executions... But these words apply to the transgressors of the law of Christ and their punishment is the death of damnation. Jesus Christ sent St. Paul to call the transgressors to the judgment of death and repentance... And St. Paul preached to them repentance, giving himself for an example, that he was a murderer, and an enemy, and that (in spite of that) Christ Jesus showed him supreme patience, accepting him into his grace for the edification of those who are to believe in the Son of God and to repent for that for which they deserve death, and even hell... The doctors have built a false foundation on these words with which they murder people, having perverted these words into a law for the spilling of free blood; and they gave this law as a testament to state authorities.

169

CHAPTER 72

THE ARGUMENTS OF AEGIDIUS CARLERII

(CONTINUED)

The second justification of war is also affixed to the words of Saint Paul who says:

If you do wrong, be afraid, for he does not bear the sword in vain; he is the servant of God to execute his wrath on the wrong-doer.

[Paul speaks of the civil authority; in his case it was personalized by Emperor Nero.] And Paul admits that Nero with his sword is a servant of God, and an executioner of God's anger. [Yet Nero used his sword even against Paul condemning him to death. The apostle committed no wrong and yet the Emperor killed him. And here come the Church's obedient apologists who say, "He did not kill; it was the law that killed."] Accordingly, the soldiers do not take their murders to their consciences ... because their murdering is not killing ... but simply the exercise of the law, and so a service to God... The sanctity of the great saints is removing the (stigma) of a bad conscience from (killing)...

CHAPTER 73

REFUTATION OF THE ARGUMENTS OF

ALBERTUS MAGNUS OF COLOGNE

Now we shall speak of the arguments of Albertus Magnus, a doctor; they too, will leave us disconsolate. He says that in our time there was born from our disputations, in the depths of an abyss – that is, in the depths of the devil's snares – a small frog which has the audacity to croak against the justice and the law of God, and to assume that it is in no wise and for no reason permissible to kill a man. Not only must they who refuse to do justice be chastised and called unjust, but also they must be punished and called enemies of justice... Therefore justice and discipline must muster all strength and power and arm itself against injustice and lack of discipline...

And Master Albertus goes into great details in his arguments against the little frog whose croaking is so distressing to him. And he goes on to say that every life that is taken is taken by God. He who resists God must be killed, and whoever lives unjustly rebels against God; and it is particularly the heretics and pagans who rebel against God... One must necessarily take their physical life away from them as well as their mortal soul. Eternal death must be the reward of sin, and it is more easily given with a physical death! So we ask the frog: is it allowed to go to war against the enemies of God? It is clear that in a just war all enemies of God must be killed... For if the frog says that one should not kill the enemies of God ... then the honor of God would be exterminated in retreat...

The iniquitous frog asks that the City of God be left defenseless and abandoned to robberies and violence. And, adds Master Albertus, if the worth of life should be the cause of no killing, then, it seems to us, the spiritual life is much more worthy; and the physical life should not be pardoned if the spiritual can thus be saved.

CHAPTER 74

ARGUMENTS OF ALBERTUS MAGNUS (CONTINUED)

This shows (says Albertus) what a disgrace against God and human souls are the croakings of the erring little frog. [Therefore, Albertus reasons, since the spiritual sufferings of hell are much more painful than all physical mortal woes, it is better to torture the sinners while they are alive than to have them suffer after death!] This we say about the little frogs who, under the disguise of saintliness, corrupt the faithful by their iniquity, thus damaging the vineyard of the Lord of hosts.

CHAPTER 75

ARGUMENTS OF ALBERTUS MAGNUS (CONTINUED)

All this is said by that great lord Albertus. [His wisdom shows how far the poison poured into the Church eleven hundred years ago has spread.] It is poison that has become life to the people, and the medicine used against poison itself is such a mortal venom that those who have been nurtured by poison consider injustice as a healthy state; they call that which has grown out of poison, life... If Albertus is right, then Christ and all the apostles were wrong. [But Christ and his disciples went about preaching salvation through long-suffering, patience, and humility.] The teaching of Albertus Magnus is contrary to the teaching of the apostles. He is now considered a great doctor in the field of Christian knowledge. Many a priest regards himself rich in wisdom when he preaches his reasonings to the peasants... He does not know what a poverty there is in his books, and how far they are from the apostles...

And as to the humble and suffering apostolic Christians, behold! He calls them frogs crawling out of an abyss, arrogantly croaking against the justice of God! The justice of God he makes out to be injustice, falseness, and evil.

The life of poverty is not appealing to Albertus Magnus; he prefers the life of comfort, of abundant food, of a big belly, of a red ruddy face, the life of security, sitting in a castle protected by swords, unafraid of temptations... This life appeals to Albertus more than it did even to Sylvester who was hiding in the caves and in forests... The apostles, the fools of Christ, were chased from town to town, as it is written,For your sake we are being killed all day long; we are regarded as sheep to be slaughtered.

[What the Church of Albertus is fighting for is not the justice of God but the justice of this world.]

CHAPTER 76

ARGUMENTS OF ALBERTUS MAGNUS (CONCLUSION)

The justice of revenge and of shedding blood, as adopted by the Church, is pagan and of this world. Even the Church is of this world, following in the footprints of the pagans... The Justice of Albertus shall be judged a great injustice in the eyes of God. It is therefore safer to be with the little croaking frog in prison than in freedom with the loudly howling Albertus. The crucified Jesus shall hear the weak voice of the little frog... Among all Christendom there is no executioner as ferocious as that Albertus Magnus, who opened the way to legal bloodshed, so contrary to brotherly love. He thinks it is better to kill off all transgressors than letting them live with the chance of repentance... God gives them an opportunity of repentance so that they would not die in perdition; and he says of them:

I have no pleasure in the death of the wicked, but rather in this, that the wicked man turn from his way and live.

But Albertus wants it otherwise; he wants that all be murdered.

CHAPTER 77

RESUMPTION OF THE ARGUMENTS OF AEGIDIUS CARLERII

Here I shall list again a few other propositions of Master Aegidius... For instance, among many other arguments, he says that law is given to people according to their various dispositions and characters. There are different laws for different kinds of people...

Thus adultery, which is regarded as sin and is so punished if committed by honorable burghers, ... is not punished in cities where it is tolerated for the common good of all. In order to strengthen his position he quoted old saints, such as Augustine and Jerome, who said, "Shall you empty the city of harlots and fill it with lustfulness?"

The old saints, in their concern for the well-being of the communities, provided them with legality concerning harlots, so that a town, suffering from lustfulness, might be relieved of it by communal prostitutes. The Master Aegidius confirms this with the help of the Church Doctors. [There is one type of law for honorable burghers, says Aegidius, and another type of law for harlots; the human law is so perfect that it has a provision for all mortal sins.]

[As long as things are done in accordance with the accepted laws, they are not wrong and not punishable. But Aegidius and the doctors are terribly wrong.] Did not our Lord Jesus Christ say, You have heard it was said of old, 'You shall not commit adultery.' But I say to you that everyone who looks at a woman lustfully has already committed adultery with her in his heart.

Thus, the human law is contrary to the law of Christ, because the goal of the human law is the satisfaction of the community, to which satisfaction belong all virtues and mores... The prosecution of public prostitution would only lead to secret vices, causing much discomfort in the community, and all these would offend God more than harlotry.

CHAPTER 78

ARGUMENTS OF AEGIDIUS CARLERII (CONTINUED)

[All these arguments were presented at the Council of Basel in the disputation between Aegidius and the priest Nicholas of Písek.] The Bishop defended the law of God saying that all human affairs among Christians should be carried out in accordance with the law of God ... while Aegidius learnedly defended the human laws...

He divided the people into two groups: one in which there are the perfect people, and the other composed of imperfect people... The law of God is given only to the perfect ones, but the law of men applies to the imperfect men. That law decides who should be the ruler, and takes into consideration the people's character, the customs, and the region. These human laws are for no other purpose but to serve the common good of all. Their end is the supreme good of the community. [It is the task of the human law to punish rubbery, murder, and adultery, but also to permit certain things which would not be acceptable in the law of God, if these things contribute to the common good of all – for instance: controlled harlotry, warfare, ribaldry, and usury.]

Aegidius, the learned advocate of the Church of Rome, ... knows nothing about a Christian life lived in perfection and in accordance with the law of God. [All he cares about is a smooth-running civil administration, even if it means to condone certain evils with which to insure the good favors and peaceableness of the citizenry. His proposition means catering to human weakness, greed, comfort, and false pleasures.]

However, the faith of the saints means believing in God and His law, even if it involves a stand against one's personal advantage, against comfort, against the established customs and life of the community. Rather death than choosing anything that stands against the law of God! Without the law of God faith is dead and the devil holds the scepter...

CHAPTER 79

ARGUMENTS OF AEGIDIUS CARLERII (CONTINUED)

The misled people die to goodness because they stand under the civil rule and under the blindest hypocrites who poison them continually with their venom. The people can show nothing good about them, even though they trust in them...

The rulers have first of all established their authority through the Scripture that says that they do not bear the sword in vain and that they are the servants of God to execute His wrath on the wrong-doers. And after they

175

had looked at their (role) more carefully they realized that it would not be wise for them to serve God in punishing with the sword all mortal sins against God, because then the whole Bohemian countryside would become a barren land, and very few people would be left alive.

Therefore, examining the law again, after they had subjected the people to the authority of their sword, they made the law over to suit their ends better. They eased up on the original justice, choosing a "servant of God" who, with the sword in his hand, would watch over the three sins that disturb the welfare of the community: namely robbery, murder, and adultery. [They close their eyes before other sins that are evil in the sight of God. They serve not God with their authority, but themselves.] When the servant of the Church – who thinks he is the successor of the apostles – leads the people to repentance saying that Christ has not come to save the righteous but the sinful ... he contradicts the intention of the servant with the sword who thinks he serves God by executing the sinners... If the servant of the sword cuts off the heads of the evil-doers, he deprives them of their chance of salvation... And so these two 'servants of God,' one spiritual and the other secular, stand in each other's way... The ridiculousness of this situation is often apparent. When the servant of the state leads a sinner to execution, the servant of the Church runs there trying to prevent this and to lead the sinner to repentance... The one wants to condemn to death by the judgment of St. Paul, the other wants to save by confession on the basis of the Scripture... Both claim to serve the same Lord. When men lose sight of truth they wander as blind in darkness, clutching this or that, whatever their hands can find.

Both the state and the Church depend upon the sword as their final argument. And both surpass the pagans in their querulousness, for even the pagans are more moderate in their use of the sword since they do not have to contend with so many lords and useless clergymen – knights of the Cross, abbots, bishops, popes – who all hold great dominions and lead wars as other servants of the sword... Yes, they do not bear their swords for nothing; they rob and oppress the poor working people.

And the lords have caused the division of the common people, inciting them against each other, every lord driving his people in hordes against

176

another. The lords have induced the people to murder, to march in arms, to go together in formations, to be trained with guns and other wicked weapons, and to be always prepared and ready for battle.

Through these things brotherly love has been drowned in spilled blood... The lords have corrupted the people through a multiple corruption... The people were alienated from God through the poison poured in by the Pope and Emperor... Therefore I see no truth in the reasons of the learned doctors, be they ancient or contemporary... For Jesus came as a real physician offering medicine and not poison... He came saying, Those who are well have no need of a physician, but those who are sick; I have not come to call the righteous, but sinners to repentance.

And those whom the old Law commanded to be killed for transgression, he saved from the hands of the persecutors, saying, Let him who is without sin among you be the first to throw a stone at her!

Love is the law of Christ. There are two ways, far apart from each other: the way of Christ, and the way of the Church Doctors. Who still is in doubt whom to believe is to be pitied?

CHAPTER 80

ARGUMENTS OF AEGIDIUS CARLERII (CONCLUSION)

Jesus is now very poor and he does not have multitudes following him, excepting the outcast and the unlearned... But the doctors are too rich and too famous in the world; they have begotten many servants of God with swords – that is why the entire world looks up to them.

Therefore, when a worldly-wise man beholds Christ, abandoned, dressed in the garb of poverty and full of threats of danger, they will turn away from him and follow after the doctors who serve God with great learning in cathedrals, in armies, with bailiffs, at thumbscrews, in city-halls, beneath pillories and gallows. The whole wise world is following such service of God, but only a fool will come after Christ and be ridiculed by all and sundry.

CHAPTER 81

MILITARY SERVICE AND WAR ARE

CONTRARY TO THE LAW OF CHRIST

In the following I shall show how the military service is contrary to Christ. The authorities think that the best way to get rid of contrary things is through fighting or other forms of revenge and repulsion. Therefore, they rise up against enemies with force, wage war against them, repay evil for evil, and murder them in order to establish peace – this is the whole aim of the military service. And propaganda always runs ahead of the struggle saying, "This is not for our sake, but for God's sake." God knows this propaganda, and the people know it too because, were it God's struggle, they would all be long-suffering, and accept afflictions... But the warriors' behavior shows that they are lying and that they are serving God falsely when they cannot stand a slander at home, while at the same time they take no thought of blasphemies against God.

But I have said that our Lord Jesus detests this behavior in his followers; he leaves it to the pagans and painted hypocrites in faith. But to his servants he gave a commandment to love their enemies and to do them good for evil deeds: to give them food and drink when they are hungry and thirsty, and to pray for them to God saying, "O Lord God, forgive them, for they know not what they are doing." This behavior does not incite enemies to fighting, but it tames their anger and lust for war. [They who want to live a Christian life must look for an example in Jesus Christ.] One day when the Samaritans would not receive him, James and John said to him, "Lord, do you want us to bid fire come down from heaven and consume them as Elijah once did?" But he turned and said to them, "You do not know what manner of spirit you are of; for the Son of man came not to destroy men's lives but to save them. [The follower of Jesus follows this example; the servant of the Emperor lives the old way.]

The Pope, having received temporal dominion from the Emperor, defends both by the sword, claiming by means of many texts and of sly and cunning reasonings that this is in the service of God. He covers Anti-Christ's footprints with Caesar's sword and has the Holy Spirit sitting on this new layer of sand... Laban could not find the household gods because Rachel was sitting down on them. Christ is the way and he who hides it with his sanctimoniousness commits a crime against the people who desire to take his way...

[Jesus used the way of love even when it seemed to be to his disadvantage. When the Samaritans refused him, he was more concerned about their souls than his personal prestige, and did good to them who thought evil of him. If we are his disciples, we love our enemies, forgive their evils, and pray for them, being more concerned about their souls than our bodily safety. All this is contrary to the way of the sword. The whole test of a Christian comes to this: is he willing to love his enemies?]

For, if the Christians believed in this commandment of love, and accepted it among themselves, the sword would immediately fall from their hands, all conflicts and wars would cease among them, no one would threaten another with a sword, but gracefully do good for evil; and should they be hurt and oppressed by others, they would not strike back with their sword but patiently suffer all evil, being more worried about spiritual than physical harm. But the world knew not our Savior nor is it accepting his exalted teaching. For the sword keeps on punishing transgressions... It kills people in war and otherwise.

Wars and other kinds of murder have their beginning in the hatred of the enemy and in the unwillingness to be patient with evil. Their root is in intemperate self-love and in immoderate affection for temporal possessions. And these conflicts are brought into this world because men do not trust the Son of God enough to abide by his commandments. And so they choose the evil and the bitter; for when true things perish, evil

179

weeds grow in their stead, and the sword is immediately after them with extermination.

CHAPTER 82

MILITARISM CONTRARY TO THE LAW OF CHRIST (CONTINUED)

The sword separates the Christians from God... They are united to him by following Christ's perfection. They have been redeemed together by the blood of Christ, and together they pray,Our Father who is in heaven, forgive us our debts, as we also have forgiven our debtors.

They profess one common Father and say, "forgive us – as we have forgiven." They are one with God and partakers of His goodness. If they embrace such a brotherly fellowship in the bond of love and peace, who are the old monks of exalted saintliness who want to deduce from this faith war and murder?

The pagans are no partakers of divine graces that the Christians claim, and therefore they are allowed to struggle for temporal things in accordance with their blindness and pride and avarice... But if the Christians behave thus, they are worse than the pagans. And they do not resemble even the Jews who were allowed to kill and to war by their Law; but to us killing is forbidden not only by the law but by the wrath of God as well.

CHAPTER 83

MILITARISM CONTRARY TO THE LAW OF CHRIST (CONTINUED)

The second difference between the Jewish wars and the wars conducted by misled Christians consists in this, that they made wars solely against pagans, having been forbidden to fight among themselves. For when the ten tribes seceded from the throne of David after Solomon's death, Rehoboam the son of Solomon wanted to go to war against the ten tribes, and a prophet of God said to them:Thus says the Lord: You shall not go up or fight against your kinsmen. Return every man to his house.

Therefore, if the Christians war among themselves they transgress not only against the perfect law of Christ but also against the law of the Jews...

The Christians, partaking of the same faith and having been redeemed by the same blood of Christ – thus united to him by the bond of grace – are bound to die one for another; therefore, if they kill they secede from this bond of brotherly grace and from the union of Christ's blood. They disgrace the blood of Christ...

The pagans are less evil than the Christians when they make wars among themselves because they have not known God... There is nothing more abhorrent to the sacrifice of Christ than this: to kill in anger and hatred a brother for whom Christ died in his great love.

CHAPTER 84

MILITARISM CONTRARY TO THE LAW OF CHRIST (CONTINUED)

And if there are some who object saying, "We have nothing to do with spiritual things and we cannot understand religious matters; we are plenty busy with this world and our military calling – how could we understand religious problems and enquire after them?" there is a short answer for them: if one is a Christian and takes interest in the things of this world, he is abandoning Christ and cannot understand the benefits of Christ's religion. His faith is of no avail, his baptism is of no use, and his belief in purgatory is in vain... Therefore, with their shameful sins they deny Jesus Christ. They add their cruelties to his wounds...

CHAPTER 85

MILITARISM CONTRARY TO THE LAW OF CHRIST (CONCLUSION)

[Wars among Christians are un-Christian. They are contrary to the teachings of Christ. His whole message is based on love and on not resisting evil. For a Christian to fight is a disgrace and shame since he should not be concerned about personal safety.]

The Christians who are of the world are also called the Holy Church; and because the Church is of the world, which does not accept (spiritual laws) that would spell death to the mundane (way of living), it is becoming corrupted; its end is not salvation but damnation.

CHAPTER 86

INTERPRETATION OF ROMANS 13:5-7

Saint Paul finishes his speech by saying,

Therefore, one must be subject, not only to avoid God's wrath, but also for the sake of conscience. For the same reason you also pay taxes, for the authorities are ministers of God, attending to this very thing. Pay all of them their dues: taxes to whom taxes are due, revenue to whom revenue is due, respect to whom respect is due, and honor to whom honor is due.

These words of Saint Paul make it clear that ... he is not speaking of authorities of the Christian faith but of pagans in Rome... He admonishes them to be subject not only because of wrath but also because of conscience.

First, concerning wrath, [if the subjects disobey their lord, they shall be punished by the might of the lords through imprisonments, executions, and expropriations. Pilate punished the Jews for their rebellion, and therefore

Paul admonishes the faithful not to incite the anger of Emperor Nero or other pagans who shed the blood of the Christians.]

Second, concerning conscience, [if the governing authorities do good, to resist them would mean to scorn the law of God. For God asks us to live peaceably with all, as far as it depends on us. As Christians, we live – a small minority – among pagans, and the restraining power of authority is for their good.]

CHAPTER 87

INTERPRETATION OF ROMANS 13:5-7 (CONTINUED)

[What does Paul mean by obedience to authority? Having once fallen away from the pure faith through the Donation of Constantine, the Christians now consider their state of fallenness as normal and as expressing the apostolic faith. The priests have adopted state authority and with it a pagan mode of living.] Therefore, the words of Saint Paul, addressed as they were to the congregation of believers living in Rome under a pagan power, urges them to be obedient to the existing authority.
[But this obedience to authority must not go beyond the limits of passivity; a Christian must take no active part in the government.] Christ said, The kings of the Gentiles exercise lordship over them; and those in authority over them are called benefactors. But not so with you.

Obey your lords and pay your taxes … but arrange your conduct among yourselves according to the law of Christ.

CHAPTER 88

INTERPRETATION OF ROMANS 13:5-7 (CONTINUED)

[It is the prerogative of sovereignty to collect taxes on bridges, highways, and at city gates. If a Christian minority lives in a pagan state, it must submit to this exercise of authority humbly. But it must not impose such pagan practices in its own ranks. Taxation cannot be imposed in a Christian society.]

For, can you imagine Saint Paul preaching the gospel in the Roman Empire and converting two or three thousand of the subjects of Caesar, to appoint one of them an overlord with the (authority of the) sword who would lead in a war for the faith of Christ? How ridiculous! But the masters want to give their kings a firm Biblical foundation in the faith of Christ. They say that the words of Paul establish and sanction the authority of Christian princes...

CHAPTER 89

INTERPRETATION OF ROMANS 13:5-7 (CONTINUED)

It is not true that Paul tried to introduce the right of the kings into (the system of) the people of God. He knew that in the beginning the Jews had no royal sovereignty until they asked for it, and when they got their king he proved to be the punishment for their sins. And now our Christian lords think that they have the right to rule and to oppress!

But having obtained authority they seldom look to the Scriptures for the wisdom of how to rule. They are satisfied to know that authority is good, and they find their approbation and proof in their round belly, fattened at the expense and pain of the poor working class. They do not suspect for one moment that they might rule improperly over their Christians, without the sanction of faith.

CHAPTER 90

INTERPRETATION OF ROMANS 13:5-7 (CONTINUED)

Let us now look at the authority of the king. As it is, the early Jews had no king with pagan sovereignty until the days of Samuel the prophet. Then all the elders of Israel gathered together and came to Ramah and there they said to him, Consider, you have become old, and your sons do not follow in your footsteps. Now set up for us a king to judge us like all the nations.

But the thing was evil in the sight of Samuel when they said, "Give us a king."

Nevertheless, Samuel prayed earnestly unto the Lord, and the Lord said to Samuel, "Listen to the voice of the people according to all that they say to you; for they have not rejected you, but they have rejected me from being king over them. Like all the deeds which they have done to me from the day I brought them up from Egypt even to this day, inasmuch as they have forsaken me and served other gods, so they are also doing to you; now therefore, listen to their utterance, except that you shall certainly warn them, and show them the procedure of the king who shall reign over them."

Then Samuel told all the words of the Lord to the people who were asking of him a king, and he said, "This will be the procedure of the king who shall rule over you: he will take your sons and appoint them for himself for his chariots and for his horsemen, and they shall run before his chariots, and he will appoint for himself commanders of thousands and commanders of hundreds, and some to do his plowing, to reap his harvests, and to make his implements of war and the equipment for his chariots. He will take your daughters for perfumers, for cooks, and for bakers. He will take the best of your fields, your vineyards, and your olive orchards, and give them to his servants. He will take the tenth of your grain crops and of your vineyards and give it to his eunuchs and to his servants. Then you will cry out on that day because of your king whom you will have chosen for yourselves; but the Lord will not answer you on that day!"

But the people refused to listen to the voice of Samuel, and said, "No! Let there be a king over us that we also may be like all the pagan nations!"

The Scripture tells in detail how the king introduced his authority over the Jewish people, and how his successors oppressed the Israelites. Even though God said to the Jews that they were getting what they were asking for, in his love he rebuked the wicked kings through the prophet, saying, Hear now, you princes of the house of Jacob, and rulers of the house of Israel. Is it not your place to know justice, you who hate the good and love wickedness, snatching their skin from upon them, and their flesh from upon their bones?

And the people will cry out unto the Lord, but He will not answer them, because they rejected His authority. This is His reward for their preference of a king. The kings, the princes, and all the lords have tasted the power of authority which allows them to do every injustice, to oppress the people of God; everything shall be measured, every iniquity contrary to brotherly love.

In oppressing a peasant they defile the pains of Christ. All this shall be counted and measured by God. Today, authority is a sweet affair to the king, opulent with fat and licentious in living ... to whom the word "peasant" is repugnant... But woe unto him when he shall meet the words of God face to face... Then his violent deeds shall be met with great discomforts to his well-being, and he shall cry himself blind, "Alas! Woe is me! Why has my mother ever begotten me into this world!"

When Paul commanded the Christians in Rome to pay taxes to Nero he did not contemplate to introduce among them and sanction the Neronian right to oppress and to live off the fat of the land. [When this authority was, in the end, brought into Christendom, Christianity became paganized.]

186

CHAPTER 91

INTERPRETATION OF ROMANS 13:5-7 (CONCLUSION)

First, Paul speaks of the pagan powers, and then he addresses those of the household of faith, saying,Owe no one anything, except to love one another; for he who loves his neighbor has fulfilled the law.

[This applies for that inner circle of the believers. From it the authority of the king is excluded, together with his right of fees, taxes, tolls, tithes, and customs. Here he cannot subjugate his brother. There is no fear in brotherly love, but brotherly love casts out fear.]

You do not impose a bridge-toll on your brother, for – as a Christian – you would willingly carry him across on your shoulder. True Christian faith has no need of sovereignty and authority.

The Church of Rome has allied herself with the state, and now they both drink together the blood of Christ, one from a chalice, and the other from the ground where it was spilled by the sword...

CHAPTER 92

INTERPRETATION OF 1 TIMOTHY 2:1-3

THERE CAN BE NO CHRISTIAN SOVEREIGNTY

Secular and pagan sovereignty is given Biblical foundation because, they say, Saint Paul urges supplications and prayers to be made for all men, for kings and all who are in high positions, that we may lead a quiet and peaceable life, godly and respectful in every way, for this is good, and it is acceptable in the sight of God our Savior. He seems to give a real sanction for everything that leads to manslaughter in our country; it looks as if he baptized a motley crowd of kings and noblemen, helping them with his prayers and admonishing them to defend with their swords their mother, the Holy Church, of whom they were begotten, so that she might sit on her Roman throne, leading a peaceful and contented life; nobody should wake her from her sleep behind castle fortifications.

[But if Paul really preached all this, how does it happen that so many Christians died in martyrdom during the first three hundred years? They prayed for their authorities, and yet they were killed? This shows that Paul must have given a different sense to his words than that which is today presented by the Church.]

[In his day the pagan governing authorities were inimical to the Christian communities, and when the Christians prayed for them, they only obeyed the Scriptures which commanded that they should pray for their enemies.]

[These early Christians did not have rulers from their own ranks, nor did they seek protection of the authorities through prayer. Their true sentiments are expressed in the Scripture that records their supplication to God:]

"Sovereign God, who made the heaven, the earth, the sea, and everything in them, who by the mouth of our father David, your servant, said by the Holy Spirit, "Why do the Gentiles rage and the people imagine vain things? The kings of the earth set themselves in array, and the rulers are gathered together against the Lord and against His Anointed.

"For truly in this city there were gathered together against your holy servant Jesus, whom thou anointed, both Herod and Pontius Pilate, with the Gentiles and the peoples of Israel, to do whatever your hand and your plan had predestined to take place. And now, O Lord, look upon their threats and grant that your servants may speak your word with all boldness, while you stretch out your hand to heal, and signs and wonders are performed through the name of your holy servant Jesus."

And when they had prayed, the place in which they were gathered together was shaken, and they were all filled with the Holy Spirit and spoke the word of God with boldness.

188

This example plainly shows the procedure of faith. If the blessing of peace is to come through prayer, it cannot be done better than by taming the evil rulers and their iniquities by the power of prayer… Therefore, to seek peace through temporal authorities is a worldly affair. But to mitigate the iniquity of evil rulers through a prayer of faith is a spiritual affair befitting faith. [There are many examples in the Bible to show that this is the right approach. During the days of Jewish persecutions, Esther offered this prayer to God:]

Lord, God of Abraham, who is mighty above all others, listen to the voice of those who have no other hope except in you. Liberate us from those who have no being, and do not let them mock at our fall, but turn their plan against themselves, and make an example of the man who has begun this against us. Remember, Lord, to make yourself known in this time of our affliction! King of the gods and holder of all dominion, put eloquent speech in my mouth before this lion, and change his heart to hate the man who is fighting against us, so that there may be an end of him!

[Esther knew that the injustice of evil rulers falls back on their heads.] That is why she prayed courageously to God saying, "Turn their plan against themselves!"

When the Jews were prisoners of the King of Babylon, they sent a message to the Jews of Jerusalem, saying,Pray for the life of Nebuchadnezzar, King of Babylon, and for the life of Belshazzar his son, that their days may be like the days of heaven upon the earth. And the Lord, will give us strength, … and we will live under the shadow of Nebuchadnezzar, King of Babylon, and under the shadow of Belshazzar his son, and we will serve them for a long time and find favor in their sight.

This prayer was offered by prisoners – and they prayed for the king their jailer. He was their enemy, and yet they prayed for him…

189

CHAPTER 93

INTERPRETATION OF 1 TIMOTHY 2:1-3 (CONTINUED)

With these examples in our mind, we can better understand the intention of Saint Paul and why he exhorted to pray for the governing powers... He saw the temptations that surrounded the Christians living in a pagan world... He prayed that they should not become contaminated by pagan hatreds... For Satanic hatred is most naturally inherent in the ruling people, the kings and their ilk. It consumed Saul through many wars, and multitudes fell when he fell. Today also the ruling class oppresses the subjects. But if we are good Christians we must pray to God for these haughty people, that they might be turned by Him from the power of the Satan and from fighting and rebelling against truth.

CHAPTER 94

INTERPRETATION OF 1 TIMOTHY 2:1-3 (CONCLUSION)

There are many other issues involved in the question of authority – we have governing authorities set against each other as enemies. When they are at war, one side prays for its lords, and so does the other side, each praying for its own victory. Yet both are "Christian," praying for their own causes.

The Christians of both sides are at war unjustly, and they pray to God that He may help defeat the other side. Whom shall God hear? But because both claim to be Christian and yet are at war with each other, their prayer is not a prayer of faith; God shall indeed not hear them. This is the reason why the net of faith has been so badly torn. The Christians' faith is lame; they act not as brothers but as enemies. When they pray mutually for the defeat of their foe, their prayers shall fall back upon their own heads. To pray in this way is against the intention of the words of Saint Paul. In this way many armed hordes of the same faith arrogate to themselves the right to defend the truth. And so, one horde will go to defend the old Holy

Church, and another horde will go to defend the truth of the law of God. And another shall go defending the orders of God. And another horde shall go defending the common good so that the poor people cease being exploited. And there shall go princes and kings to defend their fatherland so that their dominion may not cease. All of them lead wars against each other for the love of power and glory in the world. And all the peradventurers of these hordes call themselves Christians, and all pray alike to God saying, "Our Father who is in heaven." They all pray for the destruction of the rest, believing that they serve the cause of God when they shed their enemies' blood. And they all say the same old words, "Forgive us as we forgive them." And yet every army conscripts and assembles, not intending in the least to forgive.

Their prayers are, indeed, a great blasphemy against God. And they are contrary to the admonition of Paul to pray for all. Every one of these hordes thinks illogically; each one is getting ready to war against the others, not intending to lead a peaceful life but a marching, military life. Its prayers are not prayers of peace but prayers for its armies and successes.

[Paul did not pray for the victory of his authorities, for the success of their swords, but that all authorities might live together in peace. He prays for a peaceable life when he says, "that we may lead a quiet and peaceable life godly and respectful in every way." This is a life pleasing to God.] But the authorities of the world seek a different peace, a freedom to expand in violence and impurity, a freedom for the soldiers to go to markets to buy and to sell, to eat and drink at festivals, to fight and make merry and ribald dances. [Those who are in authority have the power to proclaim anything they want as articles of faith. Any reasoning supporting their military defenses is acceptable, and they do it in parliaments and councils, and display it on pedestals as faith for the misled people to believe. It is possible that the Church of Rome is unable to exercise justice with the great temporal dominion she has; she could not defend it against kings brandishing swords. And, so she naturally needs power.]

191

CHAPTER 95

SUMMARY

After reading what I have written, someone may object, saying that I am disparaging all power. Let him not think so – unless he wants it so. I am not holding it in disrespect but I give it the honor due. I say it is good as long as God can work through it. But I do not approve of the things that evil people do with power. I accept authority as long as it is baptized – that is the way I like to call it.

Secular authority is necessary for the governance of temporal things, useful to the world, holding it together; the world would fall apart without it. I say this using human logic, so to speak.

However, since God is the Lord of the world, capable of governing it even without this human authority, and since we presume that it is His pleasure to have the world managed through authority – that is, through rulers as his officials as it were – therefore those who hold power over this world have the obligation to rule it justly for the greatest good of all.

But can it be said about Christians that they are more honest, more disciplined through faith, and more patient than the world? By no means. Facts witness to the reality that they have abandoned God, that they have entered the world and become one with the world. Whatever the world considers praiseworthy – vanity, comfort, wealth, fancy notions, blasphemies – the Christians, too, praise with one accord, quite blatantly without shame and without conscience. We can find with difficulty one man in a thousand who does not conform himself to the world. For this reason authority is necessary for the pagan world, since a man of weak faith will not be better than a pagan. A world contrary to God must be kept within bounds by the world's sword.

But true Christians love God and their neighbors as themselves; they commit no evil by the grace of God. It is not necessary to compel them to goodness since they know better what is good than the law-imposing authority. They have a knowledge of God within, which is a knowledge

192

of His commandments and His love. Having His love within they do good to others and are just to all men in accordance with His law so that the authorities which rule the world have no occasion to find them guilty.

When faith and love die in men – the two qualities that can perform miracles – they are left in such corruption that secular sovereignty is hardly in the position to restrain them.

God has given us faith for the purpose of doing good deeds, pleasing to Him and useful to the entire world. When men fall away from faith they are seized with the passions of this world and immediately the sword directs their ways.

The sword does not always reach the transgression but the ruler all of a sudden sends a bandit with a sword; he comes from somewhere, unexpected, and proceeds to pilfer, to plunder, to arrest, to imprison, and to murder, until in the end God leaves no one unpunished by the revengeful sword.

But all this secular authority has derived its power from a false interpretation of the Scriptures; it is an interpretation espoused by the Antichrist and all his power works against Christ and his chosen ones through the medium of the secular power.

In our days, the Antichrist has corrupted our faith completely through this authority; it is but the sucked bones of the devil; and the faith is dead and with false names among the people.

And all paganism parades in clear view in the evil deeds of the people.

END OF BOOK ONE

BIBLIOGRAPHY

For the convenience of American readers the entries of Czech and Slavic books are followed by an English translation of their titles.

Original Works of Peter Chelčický

As published in Murray Wagner's biography *Petr Chelčický, A Radical Separatist in Hussite Bohemia* (Scottdale, Pa.: Herald Press, 1983). Eduard Petrů's bibliography lists fifty-six known works by Chelcický. Consult *Soupis díla Petra Chelčického* (Prague: Státní pedagogické nakladatelství, 1957) for detailed references.

Antikristova poznáne tato sú (These Are the Marks of Antichrist)

Devět kusův zlatých (Nine Pieces of Gold)

Jiná řeč o šelmě a obrazu jejiem (Another Statement on the Beast and Its Image)

Kterak ne ve všem za prvotnie církve vokazovali kněžie aneb podávali (How the Priests Have Not Preached According to the Primitive Church in All Things)

Kterak života svého nemáme milovati, ale raději nenáviděti (How We Do Not Have Love for Our Life but Prefer to Hate)

List knězi Mikulášovi (Letter to Priest Mikuláž)

List Mikuláši a Martinovi (Letter to Mikuláš and Martin)

List Mistru Janovi (Letter to Master Jan)

My blázni pro Krista (We Fools for Christ)

Nebo neposlal mě jest Kristus křtíti, ale kázati (For Christ Did Not Send Me to Baptize but to Preach)

O boji duchovním (On Spiritual Warfare)

O církvi svaté (On the Holy Church)

O milování Boha (On Love of God)

O moci světa (On the Power of the World)

O nejvyšším biskupu Pánu Kristu (On the Highest Bishop, the Lord Christ)

O očistci (On Purgatory)

O očistci pravém a jistém a nejistém (On the Truth of Purgatory, Its Certainty and Uncertainty)

O pokoře (On Humility)

O poznání sebe samého (On Recognition of Oneself)

O rotách českých (On the Czech Factions)

O rozeznání duchuov pro blud řeč (On the Differentiation of the Spirits)

O sedmi hřiešich hlavních (On the Seven Cardinal Sins)

O staré a nové víře a o obcování svatých (On the Old and New Faith and on the Fellowship of the Saints)

O svědectví (On Witnessing)

O svědomí (On Conscience)

O sělmě a obrazu jejiem (On the Beast and Its Image)

O těle božím (On the Body of Christ)

O tělu a krvi Páně (On the Body and Blood of the Lord)

O trestání srdce (On the Punishment of the Heart)

O trojiem lidu řeč (On the Triple Division of Society)

O zlých knězích (On Evil Priests)

O ztraceném synu (On the Prodigal Son)

Obrana Markoltova (Markolt's Defense)

Postilla (A Book of Sunday Meditations and Readings for the Whole Year)

Pro krádež nenie hodné člověka na smrť vydati (Man Should Not Be Given the Death Penalty for Theft)

Replika proti Mikuláši Biskupcovi (Reply to Bishop Mikuláš)

Replika proti Rokycanovi (Reply to Rokycana)

Řeč a zpráva o těle božím (Statement and Instructions on the Body of Christ)

Řeč na 20. kap. sv. Matouše (Statement on the 20th Chapter of St. Matthew)

Řeč o milování božím (Statement on the Love of God)

Řeč o základu zákonů lidských (Statement on the Foundation of Human Laws)

Řeč sv. Pavla o člověku starém a novém (Statement of St. Paul on the Old and New Man)

Řeči besední Tomáše ze Štítného (The Conversations of Tomáš Štítný)

Sieť viery (Net of Faith)

Spis proti kněžím (Writing Against the Priests)

Traktát o večeři Páně proti Biskupcovi (Exposition on the Lord's Supper Against the Bishop)

Výklad na čtenie sv. Jana v l. kap. (Exposition on the Passage from St. John, First Chapter)

Výklad na kap. 14. epištoly sv. Pavla k Římanům (Exposition on Chapter 14 of the Epistle of St. Paul to the Romans)

Výklad na Mat. 22:37-39 (Exposition on Matthew 22:37-39)

Výklad na Otčenáš (Exposition on the Lord's Prayer)

Výklad na pašiji sv. Jana (Exposition on the Passion of St. John)

Výklad na řeč so. Jana v 2. epištole (Exposition on the Statement of St. John the Second Epistle)

Výklad na řeč sv. Pavla (Exposition on the Statement of St. Paul)

Výklad na slova sv. Pavla (Epišt. k Tím., 1:5-8) (Exposition on the Words of Paul in his Epistle to Timothy 1:5-8)

Výklad Řím. 13:1-3 (Expositionof Romans 13:1-3)

Zpráva o svátostech (Instructions on the Sacraments)

197

Editions of *The Net of Faith*

Annenkov, J.S., *Siet Viery*; s českago izložil J.S. Annenkov, s predisloviem L.N. Tolstogo i s vvedeniem I.V. Jagiča. (Translated from the Czech by J.S. Annenkov, with an introduction by L.N. Tolstoy and a foreword by I.V. Jagič. Moscow: Posrednik, 1907. (Abbreviated translation).

Annenkov, J.S., and Jagič, V., editors, *Siet viery*. St.Petsrsburg: Imperial Academy of Sciences, 1893. This is the first modern critical edition of *The Net of Faith.*

Chelcžicz, Petr, *Siet wiery*, published by Chval Dubánek and printed by the Vilémov Monastery "this Thursday before All Saints Day in the 1521st year from the Birth of the Son of God." This is the first printed edition of *The Net of Faith.*

Smetánka, Emil, ed., *Sít víry Petra Chelčického*. Prague: Comenium, 1912. Also a revised new edition with enlarged introduction. Prague: Melantrich, 1929.

Tobolka, Zd., ed., *Siet viery*, "Bohemiae monumenta typographica," a facsimile reprint of the Vilémov edition of 1521. Prague: Taussig, 1925.

Vogel, Carl, *Peter Cheltschitski: Das Netz des Glaubens*. (An abbreviated translation by C. Vogel). Dachau: 1924.

Critical Editions of Chelčický's Other Works

Annenkov, J.S., ed., *Replika protiv Biskupca*, (Reply to "Biskupec," the Bishop of Tábor). St. Petersburg: Imperial Academy of Sciences, 1880.

Flajšhans, Václav, "Postilla Chelčického," (Chelčický's Postil). Prague: *Osvěta*, vol. 35.

Holinka, Rudolf, *Traktáty Petra Chelčického: O trojím lidu – O církvi svaté*. (Peter Chelčický's Tracts: About the Three Estates – About the Holy Church). 4th volume in the series "Odkaz minulosti české," Prague: Melantrich, 1940.

Jastrebov, N.V., ed., *Petra Chelčickago O trogiem lidu rzec – o duchownych a o swietskych*. (Českij tekst s vvedeniem i russkim pěrevodom. (Chelčický's "About the Threefold People." with Czech Text and Russian introduction and translation). St. Petersburg, Imperial Academy of Sciences, 1903.

Karásek, J., ed., *Petra Chelčického mensí spisy*, (Peter Chelčický's Lesser Writings, comprising). 2 vols. Prague: Comenium, 1891.

Krofta, Kamil, *Petra Chelčického O boji duchovním a O trojim lidu*. (Peter Chelčický's Spiritual Combat and Threefold People). "Světova knihovna," no.916-918. Prague: Otto, 1911.

Peschke, Erhard, ed., "Erklärung des Wortes Joh.12:25f.," "Erklärung der Worte 1.Timothy1:5-8," "Erklärung des Vaterunsers," "Von den Sakramenten," und "Vom Leibe Christi." In *Die Theologie der Böhmischen Brüder in Ihrer Frühzeit*, 2 vols. Stuttgart: Kohlhammer, 1940. An excellent study of the beginnings of the Czech Reformation. Chelčický is given considerable attention. The translations are in the 2nd vol.

Ryšánek, Fr., ed., *Výklad Petra Chelčického na podobenství o dělnících na vinici Páně*. (Peter Chelčický's Interpretation of the Parable of the Laborers on the Lord's Vineyard).

Ryšánek, Fr., ed., *Petra Chelčického "O jistém a nejistém očistci" a "O zlých kněžich" s obranou Markoltovou.* (Chelčický's "Certain and Uncertain Purgatory," "Evil Priests" and Markolt's Defense). Prague: Sbornik Pastrnkův, 1923.

Smetánka, E., ed., *Dva Traktáty: Výklad na druhou epištolu sv. Jana; O základu zákonů lidských.* (Two Tracts: Commentary on the Second Epistle of St. John; The Foundation of Human Laws). Prague: Reichel, 1932.

Smetánka, E., ed., *Petra Chelčického Postilla,* (Peter Chelčický's Postil). 2 vols. Prague: Comenium, 1900-1903.

Straka, J., ed., *Petra Chelčického Replika proti Mikuláši Biskupci Táborskému.* (Chelčický's Reply to Nicholas Bishop of Tábor. Tábor: Jihočeský sborník historický, 1930.

Literature about Chelčický

Bartoš, F.M., "Chelčický a Rokycana," (Chelčický and Rokycana), *Listy filologlické*, vol. 48. Prague.

Bartoš, F.M., "K datování Chelčického Síti víry a traktátu O šelmě a obrazu jejím," (Concerning the Dating of Chelcioky's Net of Faith and his Tract About the Beast and Its Image), *Český časopis historický*, (Czech Historical Review), vol. 20, pp. 77-80. Prague.

Bartoš, F.M., *Kdo byl Petr Chelčický?* (Who Was Peter Chelčický?). Reprint from the Jihočeský sborník historický, (South-Bohemian Historical Review), Tábor: 1946.

Bartoš, F.M., "K počatkům Petra Chelčického," (Inquiry Into the Beginnings of Peter Chelčický), *Časopis českeho musea*, (Review of the Museum of Bohemia). Prague: 1914.

Blahoslav, Jan, *O původu Jednoty bratrské a řádu v ní*, (About the Origin of the Unity of Brethren and Its Order), edited by Otakar Odložilík, Prague: Reichel, 1928.

Cedlová, M., "Náboženské názory Petra Chelčického a bratra Řehoře," (The Religious Ideas of Peter Chelčický and Brother Gregory). *Časopis českeho musea*, vol. 106.

Černý. K., "Ze spisů Chelčického," (Chelčický's Writings), *Listy filologické*, (Philological Review), vol. 25.

Chaloupecký, Václav, "Štítný a Chelčický," (Štítný and Chelčický). *Časopis matice moravské*, vol. 38. Brno: 1914.

Denis, Ernest, *Fin de l'indépendance boheme*. Vol. 1: "Georges de Podiébrad." Paris: Leroux, 1930.

Denis, Ernest, *Fin de l'indépendance boheme*. Vol. 2: "Les premiers Habsbourgs," Paris: Leroux, 1930.

Denis, Ernest, *Huss et la guerre des Hussites*. Paris: Leroux, 1935.

Friedrich, Otto, *Helden des Geistes*, Switzerland, 1936.

Goll, J., *Chelčický a Jednota v XV. století*, (Chelčický and the Unity in the-15th Century). Kamil Krofta, editor. Prague: Historický klub Klementinum, 1916.

Goll, J., "Petr Chelčický a spisy jeho," (Petr Chelčický and His Writings). *Časopis českeho musea*, Prague: 1881.

Goll, J., "Ještě jednou - kdo jest Chelčického mistr Protiva?" (Once More - Who is Chelčický's Master Protiva?) *Český časopis historický*, vol. 1:1 (1895), pp. 47-49.

Goll, J., *Quellen und Untersuchungen zur Geschichte der Böhmischen Brüder*, 2 vols. Prague: Otto, 1878 and 1882. Particularly vol. 2 with detailed study, "Peter Chelčický und seine Lehre."

Hájek, Viktor, "Chelčický nebo Luther," (Chelčický or Luther), *Kresťanaká Revue*, Prague: 1928.

Hájek, Viktor, "Co učil Petr Chelčický o křtu?" (What Did Chelčický Teach About Baptism?). *Kalich*, vol. 13. Prague.

Jastrebov, N.V., "Chelčický i Gus," (Chelčický and Hus), St .Petersburg: *Novij Sbornik*, 1905.

Jastrebov, N.V., "Náčrtek života a literární činnosti Petra Chelčického," (An Outline of the Life and Work of Peter Chelčický). St. Petersburg: *Žurnal ministerstva narodnago prosvěščenia*, pp. 224-280, 1895.

Klíma, St., "Petr Chelčický," *Kalich*, vol. 6. Prague.

Kopal, L., "P Chelčického názory o manželství, čistotě a rodině." (Peter Chelčický's Ideas Concerning Marriage, Chastity, and Family). Besedy casu, vol. 18. Prague: 1913.

Krofta, Kamil, "Kněz Jan Protiva z Nové Vsi a Chelčického Mistr Protiva," (Jan Protiva the Priest of Nova Ves and Chelčický's Master Protiva)* *Časopis českeho musea*, Prague: vol. 74.

Krofta, Kamil, *Listy z náboženských dějin českých*. (Epistles from the Czech Religious History). Prague: 1936.

Krofta, Kamil, *Duchovní odkaz husitství*. (The Spiritual legacy of Hussitism). With a reprint of an earlier study on Chelčický published in Vodniany in 1913 by the Committee to Erect a Memorial to Chelčický .(All this material is included in the *supra Listy* etc.) Prague: Svoboda, 1946.

Krofta, Kamil, "N.V. Jastrebova studie o Petru Chelčickéma jeho době," (N.V. Jastrebov's Study of Peter Chelčický and His Times), *Český časopis historický*, vol. 15.

Krofta, Kamil, "Kněz Jan Protiva z Nové Vsi a Chelčického mistr Protiva," (Jan Protiva the Priest of Nová Ves, and Chelčický's Master Protiva). *Časopis českého musea*, vol. 74.

Kubalkin, S., "Petr Chelčický, český Tolstoj XV. století," (Peter Chelčický, the Czech Tolstoy of the Fifteenth Century). Prague: *Věstník Evropy*, 1909.

Lenz, Anl., *Nástin učení Jana Amosa Komenského a učení Petra Chelčického*, (Outline of the Teaching of John Amos Comenius and Peter Chelčický). Prague: 1895.

Lenz, Anl., "Papež Řehoř VII a Petr Chelčický," (Pope Gregory VII and Peter Chelčický). *Vlast*, vol. 11.

Lenz, Anl., "Petr Chelčický a slovnik naučný," (Peter Chelčický and the Encyclopaedia), *Vlast*, vol. 13.

Lenz, Anl., "Petra Chelčického Učeni a Soustaya," (The System of the Teaching of Peter Chelčický). Prague: *Sbornik historického krouzku*, vol. 1.

Lenz, Anl., "Učeni katolické o Antikristovi a učeni Petra Chelčického o tomže, (The Catholic Teaching About the Antichrist and Peter Chelčický's Teaching about the Same). *Vlast*, vol. 12.

Lenz, Anl., *Petra Chelčického Učeni o sedmeře svátosti a poměr učeni tohoto k Janu Viklefovi*. (Peter Chelčický's Teaching About the Seven Sacraments and Its Relation to the Teaching of John Wyclif). Prague: 1889.

Lenz, Anl., *Vzájemný poměr učeni Chelčického, Jednoty Českých bratři a Táborů k nauce Valdenských, Husi a J. Viklefa*. (Mutual Relation of the Teaching of Chelčický, the Unity of Czech Brethren, and the Táborites, to the Doctrines of the Waldensians, Hus, and John Wyclif). Prague: 1895.

Lenz, Anl., "Z jakých přičin jmenuje Petr Chelčický Viklifa Protivou." (For What Reasons is Wyclif Called the Adversary by Chelčický). *Vlast*, 1917.

(Lenz was Capitular Provost of Vyšehrady, and all his writings present the Catholic point of view.)

Molnár, Amedeo, *Strážná samota Petra Chelčického*. (Peter Chelčický's Watchful (Wonderful?) Solitude). A theological study. Železný Brod: Bratrská škola, 1945.

Molnár, Enrico, C.S., "A Short Prehistory of Moravianism," *The Moravian*, vol. 88, 29-33 (July 19 – August 16, 1943). Bethlehem, PA.

Müller, Dr. Jos. Th., *Dějiny Jednoty bratrské*. (The History of the Unity of Brethren). Translated from the German original (written by the Director of the Moravian Church Archives in Herrnhut) by Dr. F.M. Bartoš. Prague: Jednota bratrská, 1923.

Müller, Dr. Jos. Th., "Starý rukopis dvou spisů Petra Chelčického," (An Old Manuscript of Two Writings of Peter Chelčický). *Český časopis historický*, vol. 13.

Navrátil, F.O., *Petr Chelčický: národohospodářský, sociologický rozbor náboženské osobnosti*. (Peter Chelčický: An Economic and Sociological Analysis of a Religious Personality). Prague: Orbis, 1929.

Novotný, V., and Urbánek, R., editors, *České dějiny*. (Czech History). A monumental work in 3 vols. Particularly 3:3: "The Era of George of Podiebrady." Prague: Laichter, 1930.

Novotný, V., "Petr Chelčický," *České hlasy*, vol.33. Prague: 1925.

Palacký, František, *Dějiny národu českého*. (History of the Czech Nation). Prague: Burs & Kohout, 1864.

Palmov, J., *Češskija bratja v svojich konfesijach*. (The Czech Brethren in Their Creeds). Moscow: 1904.

Pavlenský, W., *O Petru Chelčickém*. (About Peter Chelčický). Lwow: Žití a slovo, 1896.

Preger W., "Ueber das Verhältnis der Táboriten zu den Waldesiern des 14 Jahrhunderts," in *Abhandlungen der Bayerischen Akademie der Wissenschaften*. Munich: 1887.

Ryšanek, Fr., "Chelčického o jistém a nejistém očistci." (Chelčický's About the Certain and Uncertain Purgatory). *Slovanský sborník*. Prague: 1923.

Ryšánek, Fr., "Mistr Protiva u Chelčického," (Master Adversary in Chelčický's Writings). *Listy filologické*, vol. 42.

Smetánka, E., "K Postille Chelčického," *Listy filologické*, (A Propos Chelčický's Postil), Prague: 1930.

Spinka, Matthew, "Peter Chelčický, the Spiritual Father of the Unitas Fratrum." *Church History.* vol. 12 (December, 1943), pp. 271-291.

Stěhule, J., "Učení Petra Chelčického o lásce k bližnímu," (Peter Chelčický's Teaching about Neighborly Love). *Naše doba,* Prague: 1917.

Svoboda, M., "K otázce Chelčického Mistra Protivy," (A Propos the Question of Chelčický's Master Protiva). *Časopis českého musea,* vol. 80.

Tolstoy, L.N., *The Kingdom of God is Within You,* "The Novels and Other Works of L.N.Tolstoy." New York: Scribner's, 1900, pp. 12-22.

Wain, Nora, *Reaching for the Stars,* Boston: Little, Brown and Company, 1939, pp. 301-303.

Yogi, Carl, *Peter Cheltschitzki. Ein Prophet an der Wende der Zeiten.* Zurich: 1926.

The Czech Reformation

Bartoš, F.M., *Hledáni podstaty křesťanství v české reformaci*. (Seeking of the Essence of Christianity in the Czech Reformation). Prague: Kalich, 1939.

Bartoš, F.M., *Nicolaus de Pelhřimov et Ulricus de Znojmo*, Orationes … in Concilio Basiliensi Anno 1433. Tábor: Archivium Táboriense 1, 1935.

The Cambridge Medieval History, vol. 8: "The Close of the Middle Ages." Cambridge: University Press, 1936.

Gindely, A., *Böhmen und Mähren lm Zeitalter der Reformation*, Pt. 1, vol. 1. Prague: 1857.

Krummel, L., *Geschichte der böhmischen Reformation*. Gotha: 1866.

Lenfant, Jacques, *Histoire de la guerre des Hussites et du Concile de Basle*. (Supplt. by J. de Beausobre, Lausanne: 1745). Utrecht: Lefebure, 1731.

Martinu, Dr. Johann, *Die Waldesier und die husitische Reformation in Böhmen*. Wien: Kirsch, 1910.

Šimek, F., *Jakoubek ze Stříbra, Výklad na zjevení sv. Jana*. (Jakoubek of Stribro: Interpretation of the Revelation of St. John). Prague: 1932.

Vančura, B., Jednota bratrská. (The Unity of Brethren). Prague: Jednota bratrská, 1938.

Christian Attitudes to War

Allen, J.W., *A History of Political Thought in the Sixteenth Century*, New York, 1928.

Bainton, Roland, *The Church and War: Historic Attitudes Toward Christian Participation*. Social Action Reprint of vol. 11:1 (January 15, 1945).

Cadoux, J.C., *The Early Christian Attitude to War*. London: 1919.

Cadoux, J.C., *The Early Church and the World*. Edinburgh,1925.

Erasmus of Rotterdam, *Against War*, with an introduction by J.W. Mackail, Boston: Merrymount Press, 1907.

Erasmus of Rotterdam, *The Praise of Folly*, with a short life of the author by Hendrik Willem van Loon, New York: Classics Club, 1942.

Erdmann, Carl, *Die Entstehung des Kreuzzuggedankens*. Stuttgart: 1935.

Harnack, Adolf, *Militia Christi*. Tubingen, 1905.

Heering, G.J., *The Fall of Christianity*. Translated from the Dutch by J.W. Thompson. New York: Fellowship, 1943.

McNeil, John T., "Asceticism vs. Militarism in the Middle Ages." *Church History*, vol. 5 (1936), pp. 3-28.

Regout, Robert, *La doctrine de la guerre juste de Saint Augustin a nos jours*. Paris: 1935.

Scott, Thomas, and Scott-Craig, S.K., *Christian Attitudes to War and Peace*. New York: 1938. (Interpretation of the positions of Jesus, Augustine, Luther, and Grotius).

Thürlemann, Inés, *Erasmus von Rotterdam und Johannes Ludovicus Vives als Pazifisten*. Freiburg (Switzerland), 1932.

Other Material

The Holy Bible, King James Version.

The Complete Bible, An American Translation, the Old Testament translated by J.M. Powis Smith and a group of other scholars, the New Testament and the Apocrypha translated by Edgar J. Goodspeed. Chicago: University Press, 1941.

The New Testament, A New Translation, by James Moffatt, New edition, revised. New York: Harper and Brothers, 1935.

The New Testament, Revised Standard Version, revised 1946. New York: Tnomas Nelson & Sons, 1946.

Aquinas, Thomas, Summa Theologica, translated by the Fathers of the English Dominican Province. London: Burns Oates & Washbourne, 1916.

Babur, Zahir-ad-din, *Memoirs*. Translated by A.S. Beveridge. 2 vols. London: Luzac, 1922.

Baker, J., *A Forgotten Great Englishman: Or the Life and Work of Peter Payne the Wycliffite*. London: 1894.

Bergson, Henri, *Les deux sources de la morale et de la religion*. Paris: 1932.

Coulton, G.G., *Art and the Reformation*. New York: Knopf, 1928.

Jakubec, J., *Dějiny literatury české*. (History of the Czech Literature). 2nd ed. Prague: 1929.

Jalla, Jean, *Pierre Valdo*. Geneva: Labor, 1934.

Krofta, Kamil, *A Short History of Czechoslovakia*. Translated by Wm. Beardmore. London: Williams and Norgate, 1935.

La Boétie, Etienne de, *Anti-Dictator*, or, *Discours sur la servitude volontaire*, New York: Coluimbia University Press, 1942.

Laffan, R.G.D., *Select Documents of European History*, 2 vols. London: 1930.

Littledale, Richard Frederick, *The Petrine Claims*. London: Society for Promoting Christian Knowledge, 1889.

Lützow, Count Francis, Bohemia: *An Historical Sketch*. London: Chapman and Hall, 1895.

Mâle, Emile, *L'art religieux du XIIIe siècle en France*. 6th ed. Paris: Armand Colin, 1925.

Mancini, Girolamo, *Vita di Lorenzo Valla*. Florence: Sansoni, 1891.

Masaryk, T.G., *Světová revoluce*. (The World Revolution). Prague: Orbis, 1925.

Migne, J.P., ed., *Patrologiae Cursus Completus*. vols. 133, 59, 76, 164. Paris: Bibliotheca cleri universa, 1862-1886.

Mumford, Lewis, *The Condition of Man*. New York: Harcourt, Brace & Company, 1944.

Paetow, Louis John, *A Guide to the Study of Medieval History*. Revised Edition, prepared under the auspices of The Mediaeval Academy of America. New York: F.S. Crofts and Company, 1931.

Nejedlý, Z., *Počátky husitského zpěvu*. (The Beginnings of Hussite Song). Prague: 1907.

Peattie, Roderick, *Geography in Human Destiny*. New York: Stewart, 1940.

Poole, Reginald Lane, ed., *Iohannis Wycliffe Tractatus De civili dominio*, vols. 1-4. London; Truebner, 1885.

Rahner, Hugo, *Abendländische Kirchenfreiheit: Dokumente über Kirche und Staat im frühen Christentum*. Einsiedeln: Benzinger, 1943.

Seebohm, Frederic, *The Oxford Reformers*. London: Dent and Sons, 1914.

Singer, Charles, *From Magic to Science; Essays on the Scientific Twilight*. New York: 1928.

Shaw, George Bernard, *Saint Joan*, New York: Penguin Books, 1946.

Thiel, A., *Epistolae Romanorum Pontificum*. Braunsberg, 1868.

Toynbee, Arnold J., *A Study of History*. 2nd ed., 7 vols. London: Oxford University Press, 1945.

Voigt, G., *Enea Silvio dé Piccolomini als Papst Pius II und sein Zeitalter*. 3 vols. Berlin: 1856-1863.

Winter, Zikmund, *Dějiny kroje v zemích českých*. (History of Costume in Czech Lands). Prague: Simáček, 1893.

CPSIA information can be obtained
at www.ICGtesting.com
Printed in the USA
BVHW080028251119
564671BV00002B/99/P

9 781941 489314